HOT RODDING
For Beginners

*the text of this book is printed
on 100% recycled paper*

HOT RODDING
For Beginners

I. G. EDMONDS

Illustrations by Francis A. Chauncy

 BARNES & NOBLE BOOKS
A DIVISION OF HARPER & ROW, PUBLISHERS
New York, Evanston, San Francisco, London

To ANNETTE

A hardcover edition of this book is published by the Macrae Smith Company. It is here reprinted by arrangement.

HOT RODDING FOR BEGINNERS. Copyright © 1970 by I. G. Edmonds. All rights reserved. Printed in the United States of America. No part of this book may be used or reproduced in any manner without written permission except in the case of brief quotations embodied in critical articles and reviews. For information address Macrae Smith Company, 225 South 15th St., Philadelphia, Pa. 19102. Published simultaneously in Canada by Fitzhenry & Whiteside Limited, Toronto.

First BARNES & NOBLE BOOKS edition published 1974.

STANDARD BOOK NUMBER: 06-463415-9

CONTENTS

1	*This Is Hot Rodding*	*1*
2	*What Makes It Run?*	*15*
3	*A Heap, a Wrench, and a Place to Stand*	*31*
4	*Getting Started*	*47*
5	*More Squeeze*	*62*
6	*Take a Deep Breath*	*75*
7	*Cams, Spark, and Exhaust*	*90*
8	*Engine Swaps*	*104*
9	*Suspension*	*119*
10	*Customizing*	*128*
11	*Drag and Stock*	*148*
12	*Summing It Up*	*161*

APPENDIX

Car Chatter   *165*
Some Background Boning   *169*
Index   *173*

By the author of

MOTORCYCLING FOR BEGINNERS

HOT RODDING
For Beginners

1

THIS IS HOT RODDING

Two cars pulled up at a Los Angeles stop light.

One was a Cadillac so new it still carried the dealer's paper plates. The long hood of the slick beauty accommodated twice the cylinders of an ordinary car. The clean lines radiated power and class.

The second car was at the opposite end of the scale. The body was a Model T—a car Henry Ford gave up on over 40 years ago. Under the partial hood was a hemi-head Chrysler "Firepower" engine built in 1951. Hidden under the "channeled" body, cut low to hang over the chassis frame, were parts from a half-dozen other makes and models of obsolete automobiles. The original fenders had been bobbed to make room for "cheater slicks"—wide-tread tires with just enough tread to make their soft rubber surfaces legal on the streets.

If the driver of the Caddy noticed the car beside him at all, he probably dismissed it as an animated junk heap going someplace to give up the ghost.

But when the light changed, beauty and the beast changed places. Both drivers hit their accelerators. The heap shot ahead of the Caddy, leaving the driver of the bigger car with a foolish look on his surprised face.

Hot Rods and Hot Rodders—Defined

This did not mean that the Cadillac assembly line lay down on the job. The secret of the second car's performance was that it was a hot rod. No one has ever come up with a good definition of what a hot rod is. Until something better comes along, this will have to do: A hot rod is a car that has been modified and altered with loving care by a driver who gets a kick out of driving a car that can step out ahead of the herd.

A hot rodder is a guy who challenges the combined smart of the nation's automobile manufacturers. He says he can do a better job than Detroit. Surprisingly, he *can* do it, too. The reason is that automobile manufacturers must strike a compromise in their stock model cars. Cars cannot be designed for the best possible performance, but must be a compromise to satisfy the greatest customer demand. Mass production does not lend itself to the ultimate in performance.

Detroit knows this just as well as the hot rodder, but there isn't much that car manufacturers can do about it. The assembly line must grind out average cars for the average driver. But the hot rodder is not an average driver. He is someone—and his age range runs from boys just moving into their teens to men of seventy—who likes to tinker with engines and who has the competitive spirit that will not permit him to accept less than the best.

Just seeing a hot rod showing its heels to an ordinary car is not enough to show what this fastest-growing sport really is like. A good place to find out is a drag strip. Here one can see spread out before him all the enthusiasm and love of competition that makes hot rodding the joy that it is.

The Drag Strip—Where the Action Is

It is not possible to get a true picture from the grandstand. Let's get a "pit pass" and go down where the action is. The pit pass is a ticket to the wonderful world of cars. We will find them built in every shape from pure stock to oddities that look like overgrown go-carts. In between are stripped downs, built-ups, "funny cars," and fiber-glass creations that look like they were freighted in from outer space in a little green man's flying saucer. All of these oddi-

This Is Hot Rodding

ties don't compete against each other, of course. There are different divisions into which each fit.

The engines—sorry, "mills"—on these cars are even more assorted than their bodies. There is scarcely one that the original assembler would still recognize as resembling his work. Headers, stacks, dual carbs, blowers, and what-have-yous have altered appearances and changed configurations and, hopefully, added a fraction more power.

Weaving through the rainbow riot of fanciful paint and glittering chrome on the machines are monogrammed jackets and decorated T-shirts of owners, drivers, and pit crews. Occasionally one will see a miniskirted girl. It is not completely a man's world.

The talk in this world of cars is as strange as the machines. The size of an engine is expressed in "cubes." Types of mills come out as "hemi-heads," "flatheads," or "four-bangers." There is a lot of talk of horses, but they are not the ones the "Bonanza" boys ride on TV.

On the whole these people are the class who as kids had to tear up every toy to see what made it work. Now they have just grown bigger. They have switched from toys to cars, tearing them down to see what will make them work better.

Off from the pit area is the drag strip itself. Here the contestants run in pairs. The test is for acceleration. The idea is to see how fast they can go from a dead stop to all that can be squeezed out of the motor in a quarter-mile run. You have exactly 1,320 feet in which to prove that your idea of squeezing performance from a car is better than the next man's.

The Drag Race

The race begins with the cars on line, quivering under the throbbing power of their souped-up engines. In the pit other drivers pause in their work to expertly size up the competition.

The helmeted drivers in the competing cars keep their eyes on the "Christmas tree." This line of lights will flash on one at a time until the final one glows green. This is the

4 ○ **Hot Rodding for Beginners**

signal to start. However, there is a saying among experienced veterans of the drag strip: "If you see the green, you've lost the race."

"You can't jump the light by starting on the final yellow or you'll be disqualified," a driver explained. "But you can't wait for the green either or you'll be choking on the other man's exhaust. This game is packed with tough competitors. Every fraction of a second is precious. You must develop the knack of splitting between the two, so to speak.

"The guy who coined the phrase 'He who hesitates is lost' wasn't a drag racer, but he could have been. He had the right idea. You have only about seven seconds from the time you hit the gas until you pop your drag chute. That doesn't leave any time for sitting around admiring the crowd. Buddy, this race is for movers. You've got to learn to move with the best of them."

The cars start with a wild roar and pouring smoke. The slicks—treadless soft rubber tires—claw at the track. The cars shoot forward. Then in seven seconds the race is over. The crowd settles back in its seats. Two more cars are pushed to the starting line. A new team is ready to go. There is no faster sport. "Blink," they say, "and you miss half the race!"

Two competitors flash past the "Christmas tree"—the starting lights—at the start of an elimination run at a drag race. They are running in the Stock Class, which permits only a minimum of changes. The Mustang in the foreground has gotten the edge on his competitor by getting off the line first. In a race timed in seconds, such an advantage often means the difference between winning and losing.

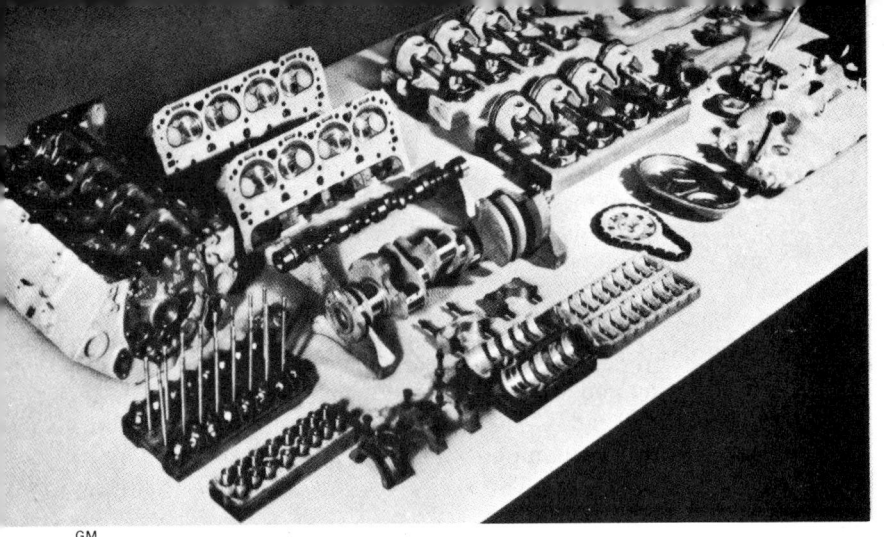

GM

These major parts of the Camaro 302-cubic-inch V-8 engine are an example of some of the critical components that hot rodders can modify and alter in their quest for peak performance.

The Number One Spectator Sport?

This swift pace just suits today's fast-moving world. This is proven by the way the sport is growing. The National Hot Rod Association (NHRA) claims that drag racing draws more than four million spectators a year and may soon become the number one spectator sport. Observers claim that it will double attendance figures in the next ten years and that the number of drivers will triple.

There is money to be made in hot-rod racing, whether it is on the drag strip or in stock cars—"gold," contestants call it in their individual car chatter. But as one walks through the pits observing the action before a race, he comes away with the feeling that most of the contestants never expect to make enough to pay for their cars. They are in it because they love it. The money is fine, but it isn't the total answer to the reason these drivers follow the tracks.

Another thing one notices in the pits is that this must be among the world's friendliest sports. In horse racing one does not see a jockey giving tips to a rival. Nor are you likely to see a New York Mets pitcher advising a Baltimore Orioles hurler how to get out of a tight spot. But you can see the equivalent at hot-rod meets and drag races. Nowhere else in sport is there a group so willing to lend a hand to fellow enthusiasts and to give help to a beginner.

Two Kinds of Hot Rods

Hot rodding can be split into two major divisions. One is the street/strip rod. This is a car that has been souped up enough to join in competitions, but is still not too hot to drive on city streets. The other is the strictly competition car.

The latter type varies considerably. Many cars are rebuilt to do just one job and are useless for any other purpose. Some drag racers are no more than a few pieces of welded tubing, a steering gear, wheels, engine, seat for the driver, and a drag chute for stopping. In their search for means of reducing weight, dragster owners have entered a competition to see how much of a normal car they can do without. Some even threw out the radiator. After all, the dragster only has to run for seven seconds or so. The water in the block will keep it from burning up that long. It can be readily seen that such cars could not possibly run beyond their destined quarter-mile. Everything has been sacrificed for that one flash of speed.

This, of course, is postgraduate hot rodding. It is for the expert and the veteran. Fortunately, organized hot rodding includes a place for everyone, beginner as well as old-timer. The National Hot Rod Association rules provide room for everyone.

Hot rodding was started by teen-agers in jalopies, but now it has gone Big Time. The really top-class racers cost thousands of dollars, and the drivers are frequently sponsored by some of the biggest automobile companies seeking publicity for their products. Even so, the men who control competition remember who invented the sport and who will be the next generation of top-class drivers. For that reason NRHA competition is divided into 27 classes. Regardless of

A wonderful way to break into drag racing is to work as a member of a pit crew. Here members of a crew supporting a "funny car" talk over plans just before the start of a drag competition at the Orange County International Raceway in California.

your car type, from street job to funny car to a deluxe job, there is a place for you.

How to Break In

The way to take your place in this lineup is first of all to get to know cars. You don't become a competition driver —and that is the ultimate goal—just by getting behind a wheel. First you must learn all you can absorb about automobiles and how they work. Then you learn how to improve on them. By this time you are a hot rodder. Perhaps your first job is a "street" car—a conventional passenger model. It looks good, steps out well, and gives a definite sense of satisfaction to drive. The next step is to want to test it out against other cars. How else can you really determine what you have accomplished? The hot-rodding road always leads ultimately to the tracks.

Usually a young man wanting to enter drag or stock-car races faces considerable family opposition. The complaint is usually that racing is too dangerous. Almost to a man drivers will tell you that racing is safer than ordinary freeway driving. This is true because cars are in better shape. Each one must pass a technical inspection. The drivers understand their cars and know that the other driver is an expert too. On the freeways and streets there is no telling what kind of idiot is in the car ahead or the one behind. The racing safety rules are set up to handle all situations and it is goodby Joe to any driver who thinks he is too big to drive by the rules.

Organized hot rodding survives on the theory that racing is fun. There is something about hospitals and funeral homes that put a damper on joy. As a result both NRHA and NASCAR, which sanctions stock-car racing, have no sense of humor when its stiff, carefully considered safety rules are broken.

Early Days of Hot Rodding

Hot rodding is no longer a synonym for recklessness. It was not always so. There was a time not long ago when *hot rodder* was hardly a respectable term to the average citizen. The general public opinion, amply shared by the police, was that a hot rodder would have to improve before he could be classed as an ordinary juvenile delinquent.

This was the time of wild drag races in the city streets when reckless drivers endangered life and property, of unmuffled motors that shattered a neighborhood's nerves, of suicidal games of "chicken" on the open highways.

Sepulveda Boulevard in Southeast Los Angeles became virtually a race track. Another section of street near Atlantic Boulevard was especially favored. It was wide-open country then and the illegal racers could see the police coming far enough away to scoot for cover.

In the early 1930's police opposition and the size of hot rodding forced drivers to seek wider fields. They found them on the hard-packed dry lakes that dot Southern California's high desert.

The particular favorite was Muroc, a desolate place about a hundred miles from Los Angeles. Although to this day most people assume it was named for the Muroc Indians, it so happens that there is no such tribe. Muroc is Corum spelled backward. The Corum brothers tried to homestead the area in 1911 and left their name on the lake. By the time the hot rodders came in the mid-1930's there was a general store in the vicinity and a small Army detachment who looked after the Muroc Army Bombing Ground used by the Air Corps. The hot rodders didn't bother the Army and the Army left them alone.

Some of these early meets were murderous. Car after car crashed, upsetting, sideswiping, and hitting each other head on. The number of deaths grew so alarmingly that the State of California threatened to outlaw all dry-lake racing.

These original hot rodders may have been a bit reckless, but they were not stupid. Dumbbells could never have gotten what they got out of Model T's and junkyard Chevvies. They realized that it was smarter to police themselves than to have the State of California do it for them.

Hot Rodding Gets Organized

Several car clubs got together to bring things under control. This helped, but wasn't the complete answer. Then they formed the Southern California Timing Association. Now at last there was an organization strong enough to make and enforce safety rules. In addition, there was the added bonus that records and times run could now be made official.

The SCTA, of course, only operated in Southern California, but the idea spread to other sections of the country. The sharp boys started talking about a national organization.

Then World War II brought hot rodding to a brake-screeching halt. Car production stopped except for military vehicles. The draft and enlistment offices grabbed off the drivers. Then gas and tire rationing completely cut off the hot rodders' ignitions.

After the war the sport came back with the acceleration of a dragster, but instead of a short run it settled down to a long road race that gets hotter every year.

For a while it appeared that the drivers were bent on running themselves out of business quick. The SCTA got back in business on the dry lakes, but a new crop of youngsters took over the streets that SCTA clubs had long since abandoned. Public opinion was wrathful. California was again threatening to outlaw hopped-up cars.

Needed—A New Public Image

The SCTA again went into business trying to head off trouble just as it had done before the war. Officials decided that the organization had to be expanded to take in the newcomers and provide sufficient meets and activities. This would draw the cars off the streets. Stiff rules would bar any member from street racing or out he went. If the organization was sufficiently strong and its activities sufficiently worthwhile, the wild boys could not afford not to be members. This would stop outlaw driving on city streets where it was actually endangering lives.

It worked. Interest in hot rodding continued to sweep the country, but the general public still looked upon drivers as a group that would end up in jail or in the graveyard. SCTA had already done a magnificent job in working to get drag strips built. Now they took on the even tougher task of changing hot rodding's bad image before the public.

The National Hot Rod Association

In 1950 the major Western clubs formed the American Hot Rod Conference, but it did not catch on. The following year, spurred by publicity in *Hot Rod* magazine, the National Hot Rod Association was formed. At first the Association devoted itself directly to helping clubs, but it gradually became apparent that the great interest lay in drag racing.

To further this interest the Association organized what it called Safety Safaris. A four-man team from NHRA started off on cross-country tours as "missionaries" to the "foreign fields." Their main job was to spread the word about their sport in talks with police and civic groups. At the same time they helped local timing associations to stage rallys and races.

From this point on hot rodding gained respectability. More and more drag strips were built and spectator interest grew.

The reason for the ballooning interest is simple enough.

This Is Hot Rodding ○ 11

There are few things that have more interest to American men than automobiles. The car is a part of our lives. It is both a necessity and a luxury. A car-less person is trapped. It is little wonder then that every young man looks forward to owning his first car as an initial step to freedom.

This is not just true of the present generation. Dad felt the same way. His eyes lighted at the sight of a Stutz Bearcat the way his son wishes for a Ferrari. The automobile is an inseparable part of our lives and it is natural that the American competitive spirit makes every owner want his car to be better than his neighbors'. Usually this takes the form of switching to something bigger each year. The hot

This exotic creation shows how far hot rodding has come from its dubious early days. Bob Hankins, renowned drag racer, climbs into a protective suit before racing his top fuel dragster, Blue Blazer. Note the added safety feature of the padded roll bars over the cockpit located above the rear wheels. The colorful Blue Blazer is not only a top contender; it is also a crowd pleaser with its unusual design.

rodder, on the other hand, looks for performance. He knows that the stock model off the showroom floor can never be better than average. And average in any dictionary is less than the very best.

Souping, hopping up, supertuning—call it what you will—is the way to get this extra performance. It is what turns the average heap into a competition beauty that steps right out in front of the pack.

What It Takes

Turning a car into a hot rod is more than twisting a few bolts and tacking on an expensive gadget or two. The chrome is just for show. What really means something is what the mill will put out. This means that the successful hot rodder has to be a mechanic first and a hot rodder second. You can't build a hot rod *until* you become a mechanic, and you can't keep one hot—even if it is a gift already tuned to perfection—*unless* you are a mechanic.

Fortunately the basic principles of the gasoline combustion engine are simple. It doesn't take long to learn enough to get by. After that it is just a matter of getting better and better as one's experience grows. This may seem so rudimentary that it is ridiculous to mention it. Even so, time and again we have seen a young man or a group of friends start out with enough enthusiasm to win the Indianapolis 500 and then seen that enthusiasm melt away as frustrations and difficulties arise. Most of these could have been avoided if the beginners had taken the trouble to learn the basic principles of automobiles.

As to how one learns to work on cars, I remember vividly watching my father struggling to get the head back on an antique Studebaker that would have been better left in a junkyard than wheeled out on the highway. We were broken down on a dirt road somewhere in the Texas Panhandle. Clouds were piling up like those Noah must have seen the day before the Deluge. By some miracle of mechanics we got going in time to avoid the downpour. I was all of six years old and remember being greatly impressed. I asked how I could learn to fix cars myself.

Except for an occasional gal like the famous "Drag-on Lady," girls do not drive dragsters. However a growing number crowd the grandstands to watch. They also can be seen in the pits. Here several girls join their drag racing schoolmates around the class entry which their automobile course instructor is tuning up just before it runs in the Ford Scholarship Race, at the Orange County International Raceway, California.

He gave me a half-exasperated, half-amused look and said: "It's easy. Just buy a junk heap like this one. You'll learn then because you'll *have* to!"

You Can't Skip the Mechanics

This is true. Quite a lot of us learned about fixing cars this way. However, it is not the best advice. Learning by trial and error teaches you only about the equipment you have. Each car and each engine has its own peculiarities. This is true among individual cars of the same model. Two can come off the assembly line right behind each other. One can be a peach and the other a lemon.

The best beginning a future hot rodder can make is to take a high school or trade school course in automobile mechanics. Neither of them will make you a hot rodder, but either will provide the solid basis upon which good hot rodding is built. Schooling of this kind is not absolutely essential. Many make it through the trial-and-error method ways, but they are doing it the hard way.

All internal combustion engines used in automobiles work on the same basic principle, although they vary widely in details. The first thing a beginner must learn is what this principle is. We can sum it up as the *cycle of operation*. The cycle of operation is a blow-by-blow description of what happens in a mill when the gears grind.

It stands to reason that when you know what an engine is *supposed* to do, if it doesn't do it you only have to trace over the cycle of operation until you find out what particular part is not pulling its weight.

This is what we do if the thing breaks down. It is also what we do to soup it up. First we "blueprint" the engine —meaning we find out just exactly what it was supposed to do when it came off the assembly line. Then we start tinkering with the things that go on in the cycle of operation to make things go better.

Sounds simple, doesn't it? Actually it is simple. There are problems, of course, but if you are real hot-rodding material, solving these kind of problems is part of the fun.

And so as a beginning, let's take a look inside a mill and see what goes on. Once this is understood, the job of squeezing "a few more horses" out of the engine will get off to a wheel spinning start.

2

WHAT MAKES IT RUN?

Probably the greatest enemy the horse ever had was a couple of bicycle makers named Frank and Charles Duryea. Charles had some original ideas about using a machine to replace Old Dobbin between the shafts of the family buggy. So with Charles' ideas and brother Frank's enthusiasm, they came up with what they first called a "horseless wagon."

How the Automobile Got Invented

They were a trifle optimistic. Their first effort looked more like a buggy than a wagon and the name was downgraded to a "horseless carriage."

Building the carriage part was no problem for the bicycle makers. The big problem was an engine to replace the horse. They finally settled on the "four-stroke" engine improved and popularized some years earlier by a German schoolteacher named Nikolaus August Otto.

The idea of the four-stroke engine was invented by the Frenchman Alphonse Beau de Rochas in 1862. Otto's improvements in 1878 caused his name to be attached to it.

The original patents described the engine as "a block of metal in which are set round holes called 'cylinders.' These holes serve as receptacles for fuel."

The fuel used by Otto was illuminating gas. The gas was kept in the cylinders by tight-fitting pistons which were connected to a crankshaft by connecting rods. The top was capped with a cylinder head. A spark ignited the gas in the cylinder. Expanding gases from the burning fuel pushed the cylinder down. This force transmitted through the connecting rod forced the crankshaft to turn.

This is exactly what still happens inside an internal combustion gasoline engine used in today's automobiles. However, just burning gas in the cylinders is not sufficient to develop power enough to run a car. De Rochas found that increased power could be developed by compressing the gas before it was burned in the cylinder.

Compression was thus the answer. It's still the answer today, for one of the ways to soup up an engine is to increase its compression.

The need to compress the fuel gas led De Rochas to the "four-stroke" cycle. The up-and-down movements of the piston in the cylinder is called a *stroke*. In the four-stroke-cycle engine it takes two up and two down movements of the piston to make one power cycle.

Gasoline and Compression

In adapting the Otto four-stroke-cycle engine to their horseless carriage, the Duryea brothers decided upon gasoline as their fuel in place of Otto's illuminating gas. In 1892, when the brothers produced their first successful car, gasoline was a waste product of kerosene manufacturing. There was absolutely no use for it and refiners were dumping the stuff in streams to get rid of it.

Gasoline is a liquid, and the four-stroke Otto engine has to burn gas. In his first tests Charles Duryea used a perfume atomizer to vaporize the gasoline as he shot it into the cylinders. When this worked, he then invented the carburetor as we know it today. Liquid gasoline is pumped from the fuel tank to the carburetor where it is mixed with air. The gaseous mixture goes into the intake manifold. Intake valves open and the explosive mixture is drawn into the cylinders.

Now here is where the "four stroke" business that gives the engine its name comes in:

● *Stroke One*—The piston is as high in the cylinder bore as it can rise. This is "top dead center." There is no fuel in

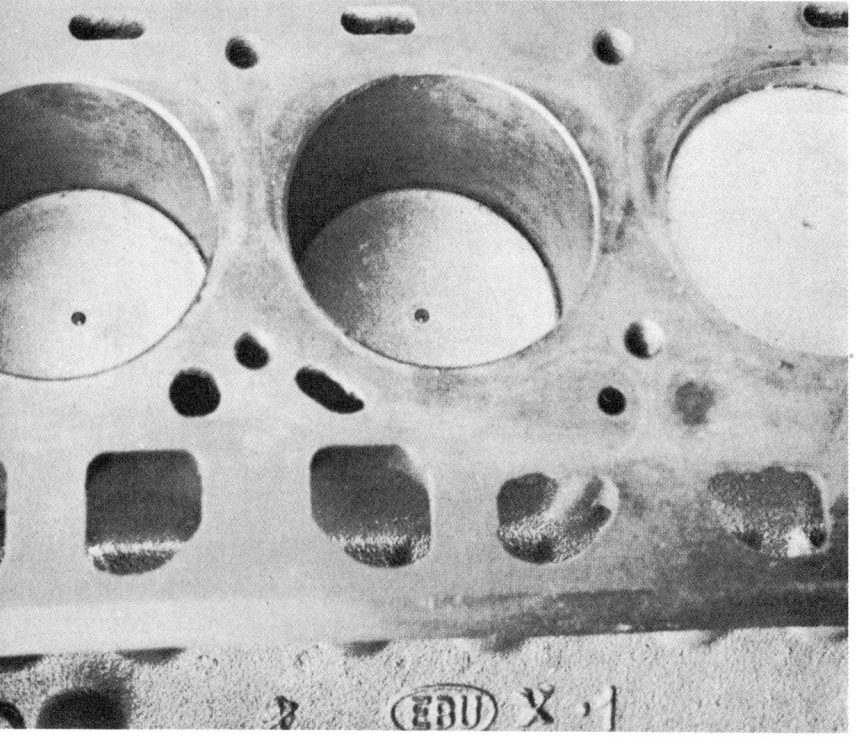

This Ford block shows what happens when the pistons rise. The piston at right is almost at top dead center. The one in the center is near bottom dead center, and the one at left is beginning to rise. The movement of the pistons is controlled by the grind of the crankshaft.

the cylinder head. The crankshaft revolves. The piston is pulled down. The gas intake valve opens under pressure of a camshaft. Since the rising of the piston to top dead center pushed air out of the cylinder, pressure is low as the piston goes down. And because this pressure is lower than atmospheric pressure in the intake manifold, the explosive mixture of air and gasoline vapors is drawn into the cylinder. Stroke one—the *intake stroke*—is completed when the piston descends as far as it can go. This point is known as "bottom dead center." In automobile language top dead center is abbreviated TDC and bottom dead center BDC. Both are important when we come to "stroking" an engine to change its compression.

● *Stroke Two*—The revolving crankshaft causes the piston to rise again. This is the "compression stroke." The piston rises to top dead center again. The gasoline vapor is now compressed into the shallow combustion chamber in the cylinder head. The fuel is ignited by a spark from the spark plug in the cylinder head. This spark must be properly timed to start the gas burning at just the right moment, which is slightly before the piston reaches TDC—so that the full force of the expanding gas will push against the cylinder when it reaches top dead center. This is the power that keeps the engine running. The more the gas is compressed, the greater will be the force it exerts when it burns. It is well to remember that it does *burn*. It does not explode—if the engine is running right. When it explodes, you are in trouble. When gas burns, it expands very rapidly. And it is this expansion that kicks the cylinder's piston down to turn the crankshaft. The compression stroke is completed when the piston reaches top dead center and the spark fires the mixture. At this point both the intake valve and the exhaust valve are closed.

● *Stroke Three*—In this—the "power stroke"—the terrific expansion of the burning gas forces the piston back to bottom dead center. This completes the power stroke.

● *Stroke Four*—This is the "exhaust stroke." When the pressure of the burning gases have driven the piston to bottom dead center, this is all the work we can get from this particular charge of fuel. Now the turning of the camshaft opens the exhaust valve and the rising of the piston on the fourth stroke forces the burned gases out of the cylinder into the exhaust manifold, and then into the muffler. Finally they come out the tail pipe.

Types of Mills (Engines)

This completes the four-stroke cycle. While our description has talked about a single cylinder, actually a number of cylinders work together to keep the crankshaft revolving. They range in number from one in a small motorcycle to eight (or even sixteen) in a car. If the cylinders are arranged in a straight line, the engine is known as an *in-line* engine. If arranged side by side, angling in at the bottom, the engine is called a *V-type*.

The V-engine, of which the V-8 is an outstandingly popular version, is shorter than the in-line engine. This is because the cylinders are bored four in two rows instead of eight in a line. This is a great advantage to the automobile designer because it permits using a shorter crankshaft. The short crankshaft is stronger.

Let's call time out here for a moment. One of the things an old-timer at hot rodding notices when he talks to a beginner is the new-timer's impatience. He is eager to get on with the soup course and doesn't want to wait for somebody to say grace. Yet all this preliminary stuff is important. Remember—hot rodding isn't creating something totally new. It is taking what is already there and improving it. Unless you know what is there and what it can do, how can you expect to improve it?

How to Get More Horses

Reviewing what we have discussed this far, an analysis shows that each of the steps in a car's cycle of operation can be souped up.

Let's go back to the carburetor. Its job is to mix raw gas with air to produce a vapor that will burn in the mill. One carb can produce just so much. So the soup course calls for dual carbs or even a carb for each cylinder. Velocity stacks will help ram more air into the carburetor. Or if we want to get real fancy, we might throw out the carburetor entirely and go the fuel-injection route.

Then next we consider the way the fuel mixture gets into the engine. This may call for porting or enlarging the manifold and possibly the intake valve ports. This way more fuel can be packed in at each intake cycle. After that we take a look at the camshaft. It opens and closes the intake and exhaust valves. At low speeds it lets new gas in and old gas out of the cylinders well enough, but at hot-rod speeds the valves aren't open long enough to get the maximum mixture

20 ○ *Hot Rodding for Beginners*

into the cylinders. Putting in a high-speed cam can keep the valves open longer and help this problem. If we can't get enough air at these speeds, maybe a supercharger is indicated.

Now coming back to our talk about the four-stroke cycle, we passed along the information that the amount the fuel is compressed is the key to its force when burned. This means that increasing the compression ratio will give us more power. This can be done by milling—shaving off the mating surface of the head where it joins the block. This reduces the area of the combustion chamber so that the gas is compressed into a smaller space. Then the gas will have more power when it is burned. Changing the pistons is an-

Twin carbs on a Porsche engine in a custom body are linked with a non-progressive linkage. Velocity stacks on top of the carbs aid air flow but do not protect the engine from dust.

Really top class is this Plymouth with a blower and fuel injection for AA/Fuel class competition.

22 ○ *Hot Rodding for Beginners*

other way to increase compression. A built-up area on top of the special pistons will extend into the compression chamber and give the gas mixture an extra squeeze.

These are just part of the tricks in a hot rodders' technical bag. We will get to all of them in detail. They are just thrown in here to show that we haven't forgotten that souping an engine is our main objective. What we want to do here is to point out that everything a hot rodder can do to a car is no more than an extension of what the manufacturer has put into it. There is just no substitute for knowing what that something is before we start.

What the Ignition System Does

Now up to this point we have explained how the carburetor turns the liquid gasoline into an air-charged vapor which is sucked into the engine's cylinders through the intake valves, compressed, and then burned, after which the burned gases are pushed out through the exhaust valves into the muffler and tail pipe.

We mentioned that the compressed gas mixture in the combustion chamber is set afire by an electric spark jumping across the electrodes of a spark plug. Now here is where that spark comes from.

The current is furnished by the car's battery. But this current is too weak to do its job in the cylinder, and something must be done to boost its power. This boost is the job of the coil. The high-tension coil steps up the voltage of the current so it can produce the strong spark we need.

The current goes from the high-tension coil to the distributor. This vital part gets its name from its job: it distributes the current to each of the cylinders' spark plug. Inside the distributor head are the same number of contact points as there are cylinders. A rotor spinning inside the distributor makes contact with these points or leads at the correct time to send a pulse of electricity shooting into the plug to produce the spark just a fraction of a second before the compression stroke reaches top dead center.

The current flowing through the plug jumps a short gap between the spark plug's electrodes. This is the same principle as a bolt of lightning jumping from one cloud to another. As the spark leaps this gap, it sets the compressed gas mixture afire.

This pulse of current has two strikes against it. One, it must jump the gap between the two electrodes. And two, the high compression of the gas offers resistance also. This means that the spark must be exceptionally strong to force its way from electrode to electrode.

As we mentioned, the normal battery current is too weak to do this and the coil is used to step up the current. The coil is a sealed, oil-insulated unit. Inside is an *iron core* surrounded by thousands of turns of fine wire. This wiring is known as the *secondary circuit*. Outside of it is another and heavier wiring. This is called the *primary winding*. In a typical coil the secondary winding may have 20,000 turns while the primary winding has only 200.

Now when the car's ignition key is turned on, it closes the circuit so voltage can flow from the battery through the ignition key to the coil. It flows through the primary winding of the coil. From the coil it flows on into the distributor. Here the current flow goes through two contact points and then into the *condenser* where the current is grounded.

Points and Condensers

The contact points in the distributor are made to open and close by the action of a cam called a *rubbing block*. As a shaft in the distributor revolves, this rubbing block constantly caused the breaker points to open and close. As long as the points remain *closed,* weak direct battery current flows through them into the condenser.

But when the points are open, something very remarkable happens. Earlier we mentioned that in the center of the coil is an iron core. It so happens that if several turns of electric wire are wrapped around a core of iron, the iron becomes magnetized. This is an electromagnet. The iron will be surrounded by a magnetic field as long as current flows through the wiring. Now when the points open, the circuit is broken. Since no current flows through the coil, the magnetic field about the iron core collapses. The electrons from this field

24 ○ Hot Rodding for Beginners

are pulled toward the iron core. As they pass through the thousands of winds of wire in the secondary wiring, they set up a very high voltage in these wires. This high-tension current—it may reach 25,000 or more volts—surges through the high-tension wire leading to the distributor cap where it is routed by the rotor to a spark plug.

When the magnetic lines of force collapse, the condenser absorbs the electrical current in the primary circuit. This keeps the contact points from arcing and pitting.

It can be seen then that the contact points and the condenser are vital parts of the car. Coils don't usually give much trouble, but burned points or a faulty condenser can cause serious loss of power and even engine failure. Points will burn, wear, and pit under the best conditions. Their care will be discussed in more detail when we get around to engine tune-ups.

What the Spark Plugs Do

The next and final link in the electrical chain is the spark plugs. All the work of the battery, coil, and distributor is for nothing if the proper plug is not used and properly cared for.

The normal processes of automobile combustion leave deposits on the plugs and wear away the electrodes. This means poor performance and gas economy. Hot rodders aren't always interested in gas economy, if ever, but performance is the very heart of their hobby. We have known several hot rodders who spent a small fortune stroking, boring, and relieving their mills to tie a few more horses to it, and then put a few of those gained horses back to pasture by trying to make do with worn plugs.

Spark plugs should be cleaned and regapped every 4,000 miles at the maximum for street rods and after every race for competition vehicles. Your reward will be maximum power, better acceleration, and quicker starting. Plugs should be replaced every 10,000 miles.

Timing—Why It's Important

Before getting down to the nuts and bolts of souping up an engine, there are a couple of other points we should make

What Makes It Run? ○ 25

GM

The pistons and connecting rods are the workhorse of the power cycle.

clear. One is the all-important matter of timing. We mentioned earlier that the mixture of air and gas in the cylinder was fired by the spark *just before the piston reached top dead center.* The problem is: how far before TDC?

This is done by *timing.* And the timing must vary with the speed of the engine and the load put on it. To understand this properly, we must go back to the crankshaft. The up-and-down movement of pistons forces the crankshaft to turn. This transmits the power from the exploding gas to the crankshaft. The turning of the crankshaft is transferred either through a clutch or a fluid-type drive to the drive wheels which makes the vehicle move.

The crankshaft has another job besides transmitting power. It has to insure that the right piston gets to the top of the cylinder wall at the right time.

Here is the way this is done. The connecting rods, which join the piston to the crankshaft, are fastened to the crankshaft at the connecting-rod journals or *crankpins,* as they are usually called. These crankpin positions are all offset from the crankshaft at different angles and degrees. This means that as the crooked crankshaft turns around it will raise or lower each of the mill's pistons at a different rate. Each piston will come to top dead center at a different time. Each cylinder will fire at a different time. As the first cylinder is fired and begins descending on its exhaust stroke, the next cylinder *in the firing order* is rising to top dead center to do its work.

We have emphasized the words *in the firing order* because the cylinders do not fire one right after another in a direct line. This would put too much force on one end of the crankshaft at a time. Instead the firing is staggered along the crankshaft. The manner in which this is done varies with different engine manufacturers and is called the *firing order*. In many engines the firing order is molded onto the engine block. If not, then one should consult the manufacturer's technical manual or ask a trained mechanic who is familiar with your particular motor. Strange things can happen when a car's firing order is upset. The engine might even run backward. The pistons and cylinder walls could be ruined. The very least that could happen would be a fantastic loss of power.

In an in-line engine—one with the cylinders arranged in a straight line—the cylinders are numbered from the front to the back. The one nearest the radiator is number 1. The one nearest the firewall is number 6 or 8 or even 12, depending on the number of cylinders in a car. Eight and more cylinder in-line engines will generally be very old models. V-8 engines vary with different manufacturers. The 1967 Oldsmobile, for instance, numbers its cylinders from front to rear as 1-3-5-7 for the left bank of the V-8 and 2-4-6-8 for the right.

The typical firing order for an in-line six mill is 1-5-3-6-2-4. This means that the crankshaft will raise the number 5 cylinder to top dead center directly after number 1 cylinder fires. The number 3 cylinder will come to TDC next, and so on back to number 1 after the number 4 cylinder fires.

This firing order is determined by the design of the crankshaft. We cannot change it. Each cylinder will reach top dead center just when it is supposed to—provided we get the timing right. Timing simply means insuring that the spark jumps the plug gap exactly when it is supposed to and that the exhaust and intake valves open when they should.

Valve action is handled by valve lifters which work from the camshaft, which is run by a timing chain from a gear on the end of the crankshaft. Lobes on the camshaft strike against the tappets of the valve lifters as the cam revolves. Valve springs force the valves to follow the action of the cam lobes. They open when the lobes push against the lifters and snap close when the lobes turn.

The camshaft also controls the distributor. The shaft in the center of the distributor which turns the rotor is run by a gear on the back of the camshaft.

As this distributor rotor revolves, it makes contact with a wire running from the top of the distributor to the spark plug in each cylinder of the engine.

The rotor makes a circle around the distributor cap, sending a surge of high-tension spark through each wire in turn. It does not make a selection according to the firing order of the cylinders. This selection is made by connecting the other end of the wire to the proper plug in the firing order.

Going back to our original example of an in-line engine with a firing order of 1-5-3-6-2-4, the spark-plug wire from

A V-8 cylinder head assembly showing one bank of valves.

GM

the first contact point in the distributor head must lead to the plug in the number 1 cylinder. The second wire must lead to cylinder number 5, and then 3 and 6 and 2 and 4.

Suppose the wires get mixed? You have a mess on your hands. To get full power from an engine, we must fire the cylinder when the fuel/air mixture is fully compressed. If the firing occurs before the mixture is fully compressed, we have what is called preignition. This will rob us of some of the power we would have gotten from a higher compression of the fuel. Even worse, the expanding gases will try to force the piston back down at the same time that the turning crankshaft is trying to raise it up to top dead center.

On the other hand, if the mixture is fired after the crankshaft has turned over and the piston is going down again, we still will not get full compression. Power is lost here too.

Timing means more than just insuring that the spark is adjusted to get full benefit of cylinder compression. Other factors affect timing. One is the speed of the car. The other is the kind of gasoline used.

Advancing the Spark

As the speed increases and the pistons work faster, the spark must fire more quickly to keep up with the extra speed. In this case it is *advanced*—firing slightly earlier than at slower speeds. This is done by a centrifugal spark control that advances the timing in relation to the speed of the engine. It moves a distributor cam which caused the points in the distributor to open earlier. This results in the advance of the spark.

Another mechanism, the vacuum-advance control, advances the spark as needed at part throttle. It is operated by vacuum from the mill's intake manifold.

As for the gasoline, different ignition timing is necessary for premium and regular gasoline. Timing is rated in degrees. Regular gasoline should have its spark about three degrees before top dead center. Premium gas should have an advance of about five degrees. The timing is advanced by loosening the distributor on its shaft and rotating it slightly.

Timing Marks for Your Guidance

Timing marks are provided by the manufacturer. Some have them on the flywheel. Others are placed on the vibration dampener or on the crankshaft pulley. A stroboscopic timing light has the effect of making these rapidly rotating marks seem to stand still. The proper degree mark can then be lined up by rotating the loosened distributor until it is in line with a set pointer on the engine. Then the distributor is retightened on its shaft.

Typical timing marks may read something like this: TDC-1-2-3-4-5-6. TDC, of course, is our old friend top dead center, and the numbers stand for the number of degrees of timing before top dead center. The larger the number, the greater the degree of advance.

Generally we follow the manufacturer's recommendation for timing an engine. However, this may have to be changed if we change the gasoline octane. Octane is the antiknock rating of gasoline. If a mill is producing preignition knock—which is a first-class power loser—then the spark should be advanced or retarded until the knock disappears.

But There's a Lot More to Know

There are many other things that support the ignition and combustion cycles of an automobile engine. However, they properly belong to general car repair and upkeep. It would take a library to go into all of them in detail. Here we are concerned mainly in reviewing those items of a car's operation that will directly affect our work in hopping up the engine.

These other things need to be known. We just don't have the space here. Any young man who wants to go in for hot rodding, drag racing, stock-car racing, or just to drive for the fun of it, should work constantly to make himself a better mechanic. If your high school has a course in automobile repair, enroll as soon as you can. If they don't have room for you, listen outside the door! Read every book you can get your hands on about cars. There must be a million of them. You will find a short list of literature on this subject at the back of this book, on page 169. Talk with every mechanic who'll take the time to pass a few words with you. Join a car club. Get out where the action is.

The number of cars on the road is increasing each year. In California alone that are 57 million cars registered for driving. All this has put a premium on trained mechanics. There just aren't enough of them—really good ones, that is. Too many garages are staffed with part-changers who simply don't understand cars. Therefore a top-notch mechanic is worth his weight in gold twice over. If the average driver doesn't realize this, the men who know cars—the competition drivers—do. The pit crew and the boy with the wrench have as much to do with winning races as the Big Wheel behind the wheel.

If you go into hot rodding with the idea of having fun while you learn about cars, you are heading down a road that can lead to a highly rewarding career.

3

A HEAP, A WRENCH, AND A PLACE TO STAND

The first essential in building a hot rod is a car to work on. Once that major hurdle has been taken in stride, there are the twin problems of a place to work on it and tools to work with.

Many hot rodders don't take either of these three essentials seriously enough. They think any wreck from the junkyard, an adjustable wrench, a screwdriver, and a curbstone garage are enough if one merely has the "spirit." We like their spirit, but not their logic.

Becoming a Mechanic Isn't Easy

A hot rodder of our acquaintance told us, "Just give me a wrench, a screwdriver, and a place to stand and I'll move any wheels! Gadgets are nice, but who needs them?"

His remark reminds us of the Greek mathematician Archimedes who announced his discovery of the principle of the lever by saying, "Give me a lever and a place to stand and I'll move the world!"

Personally we think both Arky and our hot-rodding friend were exaggerating a little. It was true that one could repair a Model T with baling wire, a screwdriver, and a monkey wrench that came with the car—a wrench obviously designed by doctors who wanted to keep busy setting broken bones. But today's cars are more complicated than Henry's heroic masterpiece. And as for the curb garage, you can get away with it in some places. In others the neighbors will be calling the police to have the junk cleared off the street. (Incidentally, if you're trying to make a racehorse from a worn-out nag, they'll be doing you a favor by carting your monstrosity off to the scrap-metal heap.)

Let's start with the car. Remember, the objective of hot rodding is to improve a car's performance. The end result is to make it better than the average. If you start out with too much of a wreck, you'll spend more just getting it in average shape than you would if you had bought a little better car to start with.

Buying a Used Car

This doesn't mean that you have to start with a new Corvette right off the assembly line. It does mean that you should definitely know the condition of the car you are buying. Then you can figure the percentage, weighing what you *want* to do with what you can *afford*.

So even if the engine is a clunk, worth three cents a pound at your friendly scrap metal dealers, the car still may be just what you are looking for. How's the body? With a little customizing spruce-up here and there would it fit the bill? How about the chassis? Or the suspension? Would they make a good foundation upon which to build? If so, the buy may be a bargain.

You can take what you need off it and peddle the rest to further reduce your cost. Recently we got a call from a friend.

"Just got me a Corvair!" he yelled into the phone. "Come and help me pull it home!"

"Pull?" I said. "What kind of a buy is it that you got to pull home?"

"Never mind," he replied. "This is the greatest!"

When we got to the lot I found that my friend was wrong. It was not a Corvair. It *used* to be. Somebody had wrapped it around a telephone pole. However, the engine was unhurt and it was the mill he wanted.

He jerked the mill out. Then he sold enough salvage parts

The owner-builder says this open-rail dune buggy was built for less than $350, including a used Corvair engine. He kept the cost down by doing his own welding and making his own design. It can be converted to a dragster simply by changing the back tires to slicks and adding another roll bar to qualify for drag racing safety rules.

off the rest to recover $50 of his original $200 purchase price. The rear end could still be used and so could one of the wheels.

Next he showed up with some angle iron and pipe. These lay around the yard for a couple of weeks. Then he came home carting a rented welding kit.

Exactly seven weeks from the time I helped him drag the wreck home he took me for a bouncing ride in a hot-looking open-rail dune buggy. The whole thing cost less than $350, and I suppose that included the sales tax.

That's not the end of the story. He deliberately made an open-rail job instead of picking up one of those groovy-looking fiber-glass bodies, because he was looking at today's calendar but was seeing tomorrow. His ultimate plans call for turning his sand buggy into an open-rail dragster. Bodywise all he'll have to do is put on another roll bar, beef up some to get through the safety inspection obstacle course that NHRA sets up to insure that its drivers finish hale and hearty, and change the rear tires.

The mill has plenty of zip, but he's going the route with a full soup job. This will take a little time. However, he's going at it gradually, for he has the time and the money. Meanwhile, his former wreck doesn't sit in the garage waiting for the day of glory. He can have fun with it as he gradually builds it into just exactly what he wants.

The thing this taught me is not to worry too much about the condition of a buy, but to evaluate it in the light of what I want to do. For the average beginner in hot rodding we are talking about putting out only $350 for the total job. From that solid foundation, we can work up as far as your pocketbook is able to go.

A check along auto row the day before this chapter was written shows that the lowest-priced car on a lot started at $99. This looks like a cheap enough start. Actually you might make it even cheaper. The secondhand car dealer is a lineal descendant of the old horse trader. Both, however, trace their ancestry right back to the old Romans with their motto, *caveat emptor*—let the buyer beware.

Know What You Want Before Shopping

This does not necessarily mean that the under-a-hundred car is a bad buy if it has a hundred dollars' worth of what you want. Also the price painted in big white figures on the windshield is what he hopes will stir some interest. He doesn't always expect to get it. He'll dicker. Especially if the clunker has been cluttering up the lot for any length of time. A car that sits and sits on the lot costs him money instead of making it for him. Talk friendly and he'll forget those big white figures on the windshield.

On the other hand, if the car is a popular make that people want, you're wasting his and your time by arguing price too much.

The tricks of buying a car are as many as there are makes

of automobiles. Everyone has his favorites and is convinced that they keep him from getting stung. Just to get some different ideas, let's take a walk and ask a few opinions.

Our first stop is a friendly used-car salesman. We know him well enough to get him to talk a little. He tells us first something that common sense should have told us anyway. "A dealer can't afford to spend time fixing up a transportation car. Probably he had to take it on a trade in order to sell another car. He takes a look at the Blue Book price on that year and model and paints the figures on the windshield. Sometimes he will steam-clean the engine and rear end if there's too much oil. This might con somebody into overlooking the fact that every gasket in the blamed thing leaks. It is sold as is at an 'as is' price.

"You get what you pay for. So that means such a car is not necessarily a poor bargain. If you are a handy fixer-upper, you may be able to turn what to an average driver would be a clunk into a high-stepping machine. The secret to this is being able to size up the car, figure what's wrong, and estimate what it is going to cost you in time and work to do it," he says.

You Have to Work on It

Buying a potential hot rod is different from buying a regular car. You expect to do a lot of work on it. That is the whole idea of buying it. If the muffler is in bad shape, so what? You'll be ripping the entire exhaust system out and installing headers and a new system anyway. The same is true of the carburetor. It's got to go anyway. We'll probably need new wiring. We may want a new camshaft.

The things then we know we will replace will not worry us. However, just to make the bargaining interesting, I suppose we should scream that replacing the worn muffler will bankrupt us and installing a new carburetor will be a financial disaster.

While these things are not important, leaks and rust may be. The first place to start looking at a secondhand car is not at pretty shiny paint. Get down on your hands and knees

The paint may be shiny, but you will never know what a car's condition really is unless you take a good look underneath.

and look underneath. Not many do this. In fact, one Sunday I spent several hours at a used-car lot. Dozens of buyers and potential buyers came in that day. I do not recall seeing a single one look under the car.

Yet it is only when you get down and get under that you can get a clear idea of the condition of the body. A quick slap of paint on top can cover a world of rusty sins. What kind of condition is the suspension in? How rusty are the cross beams? What does the body look like on the other side from the paint?

Is that fresh oil on the differential housing? Does the fluid drive leak? How frayed are the brake liners? Has the frame been welded, showing that the car is a repaired wreck? This may have thrown the body out of line.

How to Look at a Car

Often in buying a car for a future hot rod, the buyer intends to swap mills anyway and is not concerned with the engine. Too often in these cases he takes the chassis for granted. The best rule, according to our salesman friend, is to look underneath. Also, he said, if you see something wrong, try to figure out what causes it. Then it is up to you to decide if this is something you can easily take care of yourself. You can save a lot of money on cars if you can do that.

There are many things that give away a car's condition. Take a look in the radiator. Any traces of oil there? If so, close the hood quick and move on to another car! The trouble might be merely due to a blown or worn head gasket—but then again it could mean a cracked block.

Look at the exhaust while someone guns the engine. Do you feel like calling the fire department? That smoke could be caused by choking a cold engine. A too-rich fuel mixture also is a smoke maker. The first cause disappears when the engine warms up. The second can be easily corrected by resetting the carburetor for a leaner mixture. If the smoke still pours out, then you have an expensive oil-burner on your hands. This could be the result of anything from sticky valves to a worn-out cylinder.

One way to help you decide is to feel the deposit inside the end of the tail pipe. A too-rich mixture leaves a heavy carbon deposit, but if the deposit is gray and greasy, then you're burning oil.

Maybe a Friend Can Help

Now give a thought to the rattles and knocks when the engine is gunned. It takes a practiced ear to pick them out and correctly pinpoint the trouble. If you don't have the experience yourself, then try to take along a friend who has. For very low-priced cars it usually isn't worth the price, but for cars upwards of $300 it isn't a bad idea to take the car to a "motor doctor" who will analyze the engine for something between $10 and $25.

But if you are on your own, here are some additional

things to watch out for. One, how does the mill jump around on idle? Jerky movements may mean it needs new plugs or a valve adjustment. That's simple. But while you're wondering about that, wonder also if this rough idling means burned valves or bad compression.

Check out the brakes. Watch the clutch, especially if you are buying a used sports car. A lot of people who don't know the basic principles of driving sports cars are butchering these engines every day. They have the money to buy them and think they're fashionable. As a result they often end up on the secondhand-car lot in pretty bad shape. Since sports cars are in great demand, they go for some pretty steep prices.

Things You Should Avoid

The best advice we can give is that if you're starting out, skip a used sports car unless your rich uncle is footing the bill. It'll cost you a mint. If all you're after is that rakish body design, you'll be better off with a hopped-up Ford 289 topped with a fiber-glass body you build yourself.

Occasionally you'll see sports cars on lots that have a surprisingly good price on them. This usually means that they are lesser-known models. They may be in good shape and a bargain, but—

Listen to this tale of woe from a friend of mine who shelled out plenty for a French Citroen. It was a bob-tail fancy machine that even sported automatic jacks. You sit in the seat and punch a button and the wheel goes up automatically. (Of course, you still have to crawl out and dirty your hands to change the tire, but one can't have everything.)

He was plenty proud of this lovely metal beast until one day something went wrong. I can't recall now what it was, but he couldn't fix it. Worse yet, he couldn't find a mechanic who would touch the car. He finally had to have it towed from Lancaster, up near the famous Muroc Lake of early hot-rodding fame, to Los Angeles to get a garage to take it.

This illustrates one of the best rules one can follow: always buy a car you can get parts for. After his Citroen fiasco, my friend swore he would never drive anything but a Ford or

Chevvie. He didn't need to become that restrictive, but it certainly helps the pocketbook to stick with the popular makes. Then you can take full advantage of the poor auto owner's discount supermarket: the junkyard.

Incidentally, just because it is called a junkyard does not mean that its merchandise is junk. In a big-city wrecking yard you are apt to find anything if you dig deep enough. Frequently—in fact usually—the operators have no idea what they have out there. Wrecks come in and are dumped day after day. The stock builds up. Ancient heaps and late models lie side by side in these metal graveyards.

Buying from Another Hot Rodder

Of course, dealers are not the only source of automobiles. Many deals are made between private owners and car seekers. Often you can get a better deal this way, especially if you know the seller and have had plenty of time to size up his car.

Most of those I've talked to claim that trying to buy a hopped-up job from another hot rodder isn't the best way to go about it. The rebuilder has put a lot more than money into his heap. He's invested a lot of love and a lot of hours. When he sticks a price on it he all too often wants a price on the love too. To him this is the greatest piece of reworked machinery in the history of the motor car, and his price often reflects his belief.

Taking over the family car when Dad finally gets ready to splurge on a new model has kept a lot of beginners solvent. Also, if the neighbors are getting ready to trade, it is often advantageous to give them what they would get for a trade-in and take the heap off their hands.

There is something far more important than getting a bargain: getting a car that can be hopped up without bankrupting you. This is another reason for tackling one of the better-known models as a beginning. Kits, reground cams, speed parts are readily available. The woes of those who don't do this are recounted in the readers' columns of every hot-rod magazine. Owners are always writing in wanting to know where in the world they can find a cam for their pride and joy. Well, they can have one especially ground, which is cash that could be better used elsewhere.

Occasionally one falls in love with a certain kind of car or model. He'll settle for nothing else. If you feel that way, then go to it. After all, the object is to have fun. FoMoCo (Ford) MoPar (Chrysler), and GM (General Motors) are the best parts for the beginner, but if you have the will, there's a way to get what you want out of your dream boat, whatever it may be.

Where Can You Work?

Once there is a car to work on, the next problem is a place to work on it. A fancy garage is not necessary. Many a wheel-spinner has come out of the family garage or a backyard.

If you are fortunate enough to have so understanding a family that you can use the garage, give a thought to beefing up the beams and rafters if you intend to do any engine swapping. I know one sad soul who started out to build a hot rod and ended up rebuilding the roof on the garage. He put a chain hoist around one of the rafters and tried to pull an engine. He knows better now.

Safety First, Last, Always

Once a place has been found to work, the next thing is to think of safety. This cannot be overemphasized. Form safety rules at the start and stick by them. Here are a few of the more self-evident that everyone should already know. Apparently they don't, however. The numerous yowls and ouches that come from garages and from under cars are proof of that.

- Always use a car stand. *Never crawl under a car that is only supported by a jack.* More people get maimed each year by this silly stunt than get hurt in actual racing.
- Be sure your wrench fits and is the right one for the job. A wrench that slips can mean a cracked collarbone instead of a souped-up car. Not only that, but

An elaborate garage is not necessary. This backyard set-up is good enough for professional results. The overhead hoist is necessary to pull engines. Tools are kept in the cabinet at left. A canvas tarp to pull over the heap will keep out dust and rain when you aren't working.

42 ○ Hot Rodding for Beginners

using the wrong tool can butcher a nut so badly that no tool can get it off. Then you may find yourself with a difficult job of extracting a broken bolt. A wrench should fit snugly. A box end wrench or a socket is less likely to slip. Be especially careful with open-end wrenches.

- Keep your tools clean. A greasy wrench greases your way to the hospital. Also, rust can weaken tools, adding to the danger of breaking.
- Watch out for toxic vapors. Never gun up an engine in a closed garage. Have *plenty* of ventilation when you clean your tools and parts, especially if you use cleaners like carbon tetrachloride.

Good safety habits must be developed. Always use a car stand. Never go under a car supported only by a jack or other insecure props.

A Heap, a Wrench, and a Place to Stand ○ 43

- Be careful where you drip your oil and grease. Wiping up is less trouble than nursing a broken leg after you slip.
- Wear industrial goggles if you do any grinding. They aren't a bad idea when you're chipping rust and sanding.
- And finally, learn to use your tools properly.

Tools and the Way They're Used

There is plenty to learn about handling tools. Even such a seemingly idiot-proof instrument as a screwdriver can cause all manner of trouble. The name indicates their proper use. They are made to drive screws with. Yet you'll find people using them as punches, scrapers, chisels, or prying instruments.

A mishandled screwdriver with a broken or rounded tip can burr a screw slot. The tip must be wide enough and thick enough to fit the slot. Also, it is easier to work with, for the properly fitting blade takes less force to keep in the slot. The tip should be flat on the end. If it isn't, then grind it so.

There are many different types of screwdrivers, and each should be used for its special purpose. Using one corner of the tipped end of a regular screwdriver to work loose a cross-slot or Phillips screw is a sure way to ruin a screw. The skin you knock off a knuckle when it slips will probably grow back, but the screw you ruin will have to be replaced.

Other tools have their peculiarities. The adjustable end wrench is a very handy tool. When nothing else will fit, it is there to do the job. However, they should never be turned so that the force is placed against the weaker adjustable jaw. This is a very common mistake. Often when working with narrow clearances, the narrower adjustable jaw will slip around a nut easier if turned over. This is just an invitation to trouble.

Another bad misuse of tools made by some beginners is to hammer the wrench handle to force a nut to break loose. Here the proper procedure is to soak the threads with a penetrating oil and let the nut set for a while. Also try a longer-handled wrench to get more torque. In general the length of a wrench should be governed by the size of the nut. A short wrench on a large bolt may not exert enough force. A wrench that is too long may exert too much force on a frozen nut. The result will be a snapped bolt and a tough extraction job.

And so on, through every tool in the box. There are too many to deal with individually. The point we want to make is that each tool has its peculiarities and its merits. The beginning mechanic should learn something about them. Entire books have been written on the proper use of tools. You will be well ahead of the pack if you take the trouble to read one of them.

Of course, before one can use tools properly he has to have them to use. The question of how many tools and what kind are very important to a beginning hot rodder. The tool problem stopped one young man of our acquaintance dead in his tracks.

"By the time I buy a car and get what parts I need," he said, "I'll have nothing left to buy what tools I need. If I buy tools, then I can't buy the car!"

What Tools You Should Buy

The way he figured his budget he expected to have about $350 coming in over the next six months that could be channeled to his dream of a hot rod. Some pretty good street rods and even hobby competition cars have been put on the road for less than this. Our answer to his complaint was: "You can do everything you really need to do on a street rod with tools that cost less than $25. Of course you can do it easier if you have more tools, but a basic set will get you started. After that you can add as you go along. Many of the special tools specified in manufacturers' technical manual are not necessary. Tool designers often get carried away. While they make things easier on some jobs, special tools can wait until we make our first million. This basic set should get you well set up in business:

A Heap, a Wrench, and a Place to Stand   ○   45

Combination wrenches, set of five
Socket wrenches, set of five, ½-inch drive
Pliers
Diagonal cutters
Feeler gauge set
Adjustable wrench
Ball-peen hammer
Spark-plug wrench—deep socket
Screwdrivers, including cross-point for Phillips screws
Hacksaw
Ignition wrenches, set

That is about all you'll need to get started in business. It is a very ordinary looking list. Most of the stuff you probably already have anyway. For some unknown reason a lot of beginners have the idea that hot rodding is a new world where everything operates with exotic tools and out-of-this-world techniques. It is just plain mechanicking, and just plain tools are all you need.

There is one world of caution, however. Some foreign cars have metric bolts, and American tools graduated in inches won't fit over them. We had an English Austin once with these specifications. We had to carry a set of metric tools in the back end and loan them to mechanics everytime we wanted work done outside a large metropolitan area.

The next tool purchases should include vise-grip pliers, piston-ring compressor, socket-handle extension, socket universal joint, and—especially—a torque wrench. The torque wrench, which has a dial for measuring how much force the mechanic is putting on a nut, is becoming increasingly a must. Prices are changing all the time and it is pretty futile to talk about them in a book, but a 150-pound torque wrench will be one of the most expensive items you need to buy. The price will certainly be above $30.

Incidently, while on the subject of tool prices, it's not necessary to go bankrupt for a professional-quality set unless you intend going into the garage business. Cheaper tools will serve just as well. Quite a lot of ours were picked up on bargain counters. Also keep a weather eye out for the surplus stores. Some tremendous bargains can be picked up here at times.

An important point to remember is that you should buy only the tools you will need regularly. It is a waste of money that might better go for a hotter cam to buy expensive electric drills, test equipment, or even a chain hoist if they won't be used more than once or twice a year. Unless you are a professional you can't spend all your time tinkering with your car. There are jobs to be done, school to attend, and a life to live. Probably the average young man can't spare more than a couple of days a week to his mechanicking over a year's average.

In such cases it is better to consider renting more expensive tools and equipment instead of tying up money in something that is hardly ever used. We know one enthusiastic beginner who sank $500 in tools. They look great hanging on his garage wall, but at least half have never been used in the three years they have hung there.

The idea is, don't go overboard. Get what you need, but get them as you need them. Use them properly and you are already a long way down the road to being a successful mechanic.

4

GETTING STARTED

There is a story which may or may not be true that Henry Ford was out riding in a custom-made Lincoln limousine when he saw a man trying vainly to crank a Model T. The man who invented that classic automobile was in a jovial mood. He leaned out the window of his limousine and shouted, "Get a horse!"

This, of course, was the same cry that mocked Ford when he was getting started back in the days of the horseless carriage. After perfection of the automobile, the derisive cry fell into disuse for a number of years. Then suddenly hot rodders brought it back into popularity—but with a slight change. Their cry is: "Get *more* horses!"

Horses, Horses, Horses

What they mean is horsepower. They can never get enough of it. Automobile engines are rated according to their horsepower. The term was coined by James Watt, inventor of the condensing steam engine, who found that a dray horse could move a 33,000-pound load a distance of one foot in one minute. So if we find that a car develops 200 horsepower, it is doing the work of 200 of Mr. Watt's horses every minute.

However, when anybody talks of horsepower—and that is everybody in the automobile business—it is perfectly correct to ask, "What kind of nags are you talking about?"

As a general rule, they are talking about *brake* horsepower. There is something called *taxable horsepower* which is used by some states to figure how much your license fee will be.

While most hot rodders have gone for more powerful engines in their heaps, the VW mill has come into its own with the current interest in dune buggies and off-the-road vehicles. As a result, numerous bolt-on goodies have become available to warm up the Volks mill.

Taxable hp is determined by an SAE (Society of Automotive Engineers) formula. This formula does not give the actual horsepower. That can be determined only by actual measurement of the running engine. It does give a comparison between different cars, and that is why it is used for tax purposes.

Brake horsepower is what the crankshaft puts out. It is

Getting Started ○ 49

measured by a dynamometer. A *dynamo* is an electric generator, and the "meter" part is self-explanatory. The car's back wheels sit on two big rollers. As the wheels spin, they turn the rollers without moving the car. These rollers operate an electric generator which turns out current according to the speed of the rollers turned by the car's wheels. This output is measured. However, the electric horsepower will not be the same as the car's because some of the power is used in the machinery between the wheels and the meter. You never get energy for nothing. Some of the power had to go to operate the generator. This is taken into consideration in designing the meter. The result is the engine's *brake horsepower*.

This still does not tell us exactly what the car's real horsepower is—the horses that are actually pulling our wheels. When the manufacturer helpfully lists the brake horsepower in his engine specifications, he may be talking about *net horsepower*, which is one thing, or he may mean *gross horsepower*, which is indeed a horse of a different color.

Horsepower Gross and Net

Most manufacturers like to merely list "brake horsepower" and conveniently forget to add whether it is net or gross. Gross horsepower is determined from a bare engine with no accessories to drain off power. It must be remembered that there are no giveaway programs in mechanics. Everything must be paid for. Every pulley, belt, chain, or gadget that runs off the engine must be paid for in a share of those horses. Everything from air conditioner to smog-control device throws a rope on a horse or two. *Net horsepower* is what is left to deliver to the transmission.

This drain may be small, but it is not insignificant. The idea of hot rodding is to improve performance, and net horsepower may be as much as 15 percent less than the gross horsepower.

This can be a terrific drain in competition, which is why everything that puts a hobble on a horse has got to go. I happen to have before me right now some figures on the 1966 Rambler American engine. The manufacturer lists the brake horsepower of the 199-cubic-inch engine as 128 brake horsepower at 4,400 revolutions per minute. Upping the engine to 232 cubic inches increases the brake horsepower for the same revolutions to 155 brake horsepower. Increasing the displacement from 199 cubes to 232 cubes gives us 17 more horses. This is just about what a modern engine loses through pulling accessories.

Cubes and Compression

Maybe we had better talk for a minute about cubes and displacement. No words occur more frequently in hot-rodding chatter. They mean the same thing—the volume of the cylinder at bottom dead center. How much air-gas mixture will it hold? The more we pack in, the more force it will exert when it burns.

The term "cubes" comes from cubic inches. A 232 engine displaces 232 cubic inches of air-gas in all its cylinders. A 287 engine displaces 287 cubic inches. You do not say a car's eight cylinders *hold* 287 cubic inches of fuel. You say it *displaces* this amount.

Let us suppose that when a piston descends from top dead center to bottom dead center it moves seven inches. That is the *stroke*—seven inches. Now when the piston rises to top dead center, again, it compresses the air-gas mixture into a space of, say, one inch depth. This will vary, of course, with different engines. Then the *compression ratio*—the difference between the area in which the gas is compressed and the area of uncompressed gas—is 7 to 1.

The higher this compression ratio the greater will be the power obtained from the fuel. Everything is made up of atoms. These atoms combine with other atoms to make molecules which in turn combine to make compounds. When gas is compressed, the molecules are forced closer together so when they burn the heated gas—reaching temperatures of 4,000 degrees plus—exerts more forceful pressure.

More Compression from the Same Mill

The hot rodder's basic problem is to take whatever compression the engine designer gives him and to increase it.

Getting Started   ○   51

Older engines can gain considerable power by increasing their compression. Some of the later engines have gone about as high as they can go. As an example of how compression can vary, let's take a look at Ford's big V-8. This engine was originally introduced in 1958 as a 352-cubic-inch model. Relying on memory, it seems to me that its compression ratio was something like 8 to 1. Three years later Ford expanded the displacement to 390 cubes and gave us a 9.5-to-1 compression ratio. Then in 1966 displacement broke 400 cubes with the 410 and 427 models. Here compression was upped to 11.1 to 1.

All of this increased compression did not come from just increasing displacement. Many factors enter into it. We'll get to them after a while. Right now we are talking about compression. These remarks apply to older engines within a beginner's reach.

Back in the good old days of automobiling, car builders went strong for racing. The publicity sold cars. There was a time when Henry Ford drove his own car. Then for a number of years the selling pitch was toward the family car. Company-sponsored race cars were out of fashion. They didn't fit the image.

Now the cycle has swung back again. The image car is the performance car. Many of the tricks early hot rodders used have been grabbed up by the manufacturers. You can buy right off the floor today much that the old times from Muroc sweated and ground to get.

Right now Plymouth is bragging about its GTX's "mighty 440-cubic-inch displacement, hot camshaft, high-flow cylinder heads and 4-barrel carburetion."

Mustang was fanfared in for 1970 with "Option A: one brand new 351 4V V-8. This is the all-new Cleveland engine. It has huge (2.19-inch intakes, 1.71-inch exhausts) canted valves and a wallopping 11:1 compression ratio. Power? Three hundred big, strong bred-in-America horses."

Buick bragged about having a 455-cubic-inch 360-horsepower engine with a high-lift cam and a four-barrel carburetor "which breathes through real air scoops to increase performance."

Such figures sound like dreams to old-timers. They are dreams to owners of older cars, and to most new-car owners as well. A lot of this new high performance is not obtainable with stock models. They are obtained through buying options. Options, friend, are something you pay extra for—and often pay plenty. Even at steep prices, options are not profitable for companies. The family car is still the backbone of the industry. But as an option offered for sale, the high-performance car can qualify under NASCAR's stock-car rules. The publicity the company gets rubs off on the company's other products.

These new high-performance models are dream cars, no doubt about it. But if you're like most of us when we began falling in love with cars, you'll be able to afford a 1970 model in about 1980. The cars worked by most beginners fall between ten and twenty years old. But in spite of their age, these old horses can be made to frolic like colts.

You Have to Specialize

"The first thing you have to learn, if you seriously want to get into hot rodding, is that you are going to have to specialize," said an old-timer who began at Muroc and still has an interest in the sport despite his gray hair.

"You can't run around the streets in a racing car. You can't throttle it down. The tires are wrong. It'll bankrupt you burning gas. And so on. Nor can you run a stock-car race in a dragster. Even if the rules would permit it, you'd burn the heap up long before the checkered flag is waved in your face. Nor can you expect to run an Indy type race in a dune buggy. So, the question is, what do you want to do?"

For a beginner, the answer seems to be: a street rod. It doesn't take a lot of work, but the results can be gratifying. Here you have a compromise between transportation and top performance. This doesn't mean you are barred from competition. There are drag and stock-car race classes open to street rods. You'll be running against your own kind. If you win enough to pay for upgrading your heap into a higher competition class, you will not be the first who climbed up the competition ladder mill by mill.

For a starter let's confine our activity to these improvements:

- Raising the compression ratio.
- Adding additional carburetion, since the stock carburetor can't provide sufficient fuel for the hopped up engine.
- Improving the ignition system, since packing more fuel into the cylinders is going to mean we have to have a hotter spark.
- Reworking the exhaust, because it is just as important to get rid of the spent gases as it is to get fresh gas into the combustion chamber in the first place. Inadequate exhaust systems create back pressure that hobbles your horses.
- Then beefing up the suspension and customizing the body will complete Round One. After that, if you feel the urge, we can add a little more muscle and move into the bigger time.

Raising the Compression

Now about this problem of raising compression. We have already figured out what compression ratio is and how the higher ratios contribute to increased horsepower. So with that behind us, let's see what we can do to our own mills.

In the first place, it is not always desirable to increase an engine's compression. If this has already been done before you got it, it may not take anymore. Too much compression can cause preignition. The least that will happen then is poor performance with pinging or knocking. The worst is a damaged piston.

We cannot always depend upon the stock figures for an old engine. It may have been rebored or milled or stroked. From the outside, it's hard to tell. We need to get the head off and take a good look inside.

But first there is one very important thing to be done:

give it a tune-up. There isn't space here to go into the details of automobile tune-ups. Entire books have been written about this most important part of automobile upkeep. It will pay you to get one. *Audel's Automobile Tune-Up* is a very professional one. And then memorize it.

But First a Tune-up

As a general guide for getting the mill in percolating order before beginning to soup it up, here is a procedure outline:

- Clean and test the battery.
- Inspect and test the high-tension coil.
- Inspect and lubricate the distributor, checking the rotor for wear and the cap for cracks. Be sure they are all clean.
- Replace the points and adjust for dwell.
- Replace the condenser.
- Check the centrifugal-weight action and the vacuum advance.
- Check all wiring for frayed insulation, cracks, and loose connections. This includes the secondary high-tension wire leading from the coil to the distributor and the spark-plug wires running from the distributor to the plugs.
- Check the plug. Clean and regap. You'll probably be better off to replace them entirely.
- Adjust the carburetor.
- Also check valve clearances. If tappets are too tight, you may burn out your valves.

A very important part of the tune-up is a compression test. A compression tester cannot tell us what the compression ratio is, but it will tell us if there is trouble in the valves, rings, head gasket, or pistons.

In use, the compression tester is inserted in the empty spark-plug hole and the engine turned over with the starter 20 times. This insures that the test is made on five compression strokes. You'll remember that in a four-stroke engine only one of the four is a compression stroke.

Compression Test

A mistake a lot of mechanics make is to turn the engine over too many times. Remember that we must test every cylinder. In a V-8 engine that means that we'll be turning the engine over 160 times. The starter pulls quite a jolt of juice, and if you run it too long for each cylinder there can be a battery voltage drop before you are done. This will cause the mill to grind more slowly. The reduced rpm—revolutions per minute—can give you a false compression reading.

If the engine is in tiptop condition, the compression tester should read within 10 percent variation for each cylinder.

And the Right Test Equipment

Precise tune-up tests cannot be made without proper tune-up test equipment. Setting the timing and carburetor just by listening to the engine is fine for transportation automobiles, but the whole object of hot rodding is to go beyond that. Everything has got to be just right. This means proper test equipment.

The best thing to use is the diagnostic oscilloscope. Dancing lines on a radarlike screen tell you just about all there is to know about the way the mill is grinding. Unfortunately this electronic wizard costs around $300. If you can rent one for $5 a day from some local tool-rental place, it will be well worth the money for this initial shakedown. They come with a step-by-step manual that tells you how to connect them up and decipher the results.

If this comes too high for the budget, then the next best thing is an engine analyzer. Sears has one for $99 that not only includes the analyzer for checking out the ignition and electrical systems, but the old Wish Book also throws in a compression tester, timing light, vacuum gauge and fuel-pump tester, and a remote-control starter switch. Along with all these goodies is a 32-page manual telling you how to get along with the 50 different tests the combination is capable of. It's a bargain and, if you are going to do much work, a true friend in need.

But $99 isn't something you can always find crumpled up

and forgotten in your back pocket. So there's a beginner's tune-up kit for $13.98. (Of course, that is today's price; inflation being what it is, the price may be $15 by the time you read this.)

Your Own Compression Tester

Now if *that* is a bit steep after buying the car, a compression tester can be bought for less than five dollars and a timing light for a few cents less than that. In my opinion, you have got to have these two items.

Both items are extremely simple to use. The compression tester is a round gauge with a brass fitting at the bottom to which is attached a rubber plug. Remove the spark plugs and put the rubber adapter into the spark-plug hole. Then turn the engine over five compression strokes and read the dial.

The timing light was explained earlier. Just to review, it is focused on the timing marks on the flywheel or vibration damper, depending upon where it is located. Then the timing is advanced or retarded by loosening the distributor and rotating it slightly on its shaft until the timing marker and the proper degree mark line up.

Milling the Mill

After the mill is tuned and doing the best it can for its age and condition, we are ready to start adding horses to the team. With older flat-head engines like the Mercury and early Fords, milling was a highly popular way of increasing engine compression. A flat-head mill is one with the valves in the block. All one has to do to remove them is loosen the head bolts. Once the head is removed, the milling is done by shaving off a bit of the mating surface where the head joins the block.

What this does is to make the head's combustion chamber more shallow, reducing its volume. Then, since the swept volume remains the same, the same amount of fuel is squeezed into a smaller area. Swept volume is the space the piston moves through from top dead center to bottom dead center during a stroke.

When you raise the hood on a hot rod there is no way of predicting what strange sight you will find. This 1932 Ford now has a Chrysler mill with quad throat dual carbs. The small racing air cleaners protect the engine with less restriction on incoming air.

How much metal to mill off depends upon several factors. One is the shape of the combustion chamber. If it is shallow to begin with, then a very small cut will give a higher increase than the same cut would on a deeper chamber.

Then there is the design of the engine to consider. I knew a fellow who went at a milling job "scientifically." At least he claimed it was so.

The shape of the combustion chamber was irregular. So he filled it full of salt and then measured the salt to get the exact volume of the chamber. Then he removed small amounts of the salt until he got the level down to just what he thought would raise the mill's compression to 11:1. He then took the head down to a machine shop to have it milled down to his exact specifications.

He was very proud of the way he had figured everything out so "scientifically." He told me about it with great gusto.

However, he was in for a scientific surprise. He was working with an overhead valve (OHV) Chevvy V-8 and his cut was so deep that it interfered with his valve clearances. They couldn't open fully to let in enough fuel or let out the exhaust.

If you decide on milling a head, by all means take it to someone who specializes in this type of work. Their machinist will know how much to take off. Most of those who have had experience in head milling say that .030 inch is the maximum that should be cut.

Milling is the cheapest way to increase compression, since it is just a simple metal planing job that a good machine shop can do at a reasonable price. Prices vary across the country. You might figure on paying, say, $10 for a single in-line head and about double that for a couple of V-8 OHV's.

This is just for the milling. You won't be able to drive in and sit under a shade tree while the shop takes them off for you. At least, not at these prices. You do the dismantling.

Consult the Service Manual

Unless you are very familiar with a particular engine, having worked on it before, you should consult the Technical Service Manual for *that particular model*. Often these are available in libraries for popular models and makes. If not, then try the manufacturer. Or maybe your school shop has some you can borrow.

For the past twenty years I have personally made a point of obtaining a service manual on every car I buy—new or secondhand. The beauty of these shop manuals is that they do not talk about automotive mechanics in general, but pinpoint exactly the differences between your model and all other cars. Believe me, there are differences. These differences, small as some of them are, can all add up to a considerable difference in performance if not done correctly.

One disadvantage of shop manuals is that they were not written for beginners. They are intended to acquaint experienced mechanics with the peculiarities of a particular model. As a result, the instructions are sometimes not as complete as a beginner would like. The manual writer presupposes that the user knows more about the art of working on cars than a beginner really knows.

However, as your experience grows, the value of the service manual increases. *Motor's Auto Repair Manual* is a good companion to the shop manual but no substitute for it.

By the way, while we have that head off, don't forget to check the combustion chamber for carbon. This builds up inside the head, reducing volume and raising compression.

Since we are out to raise compression anyway, this would seem to be a natural blessing. Don't you believe it. The truth is just the opposite. Bits of carbon keep glowing after the fire should be out in the cylinder. This ignites the new fuel mixture before it is completely compressed. The result is preignition with both its power-robbing and destructive forces.

High-Compression Pistons

Another popular way to increase compression is to replace the stock pistons with high-compression types. These have special heads. Some are dome-shaped. Some have wedges of various shapes on top. All have the same purpose. The extra material on top shoves itself up into the combustion chamber and thus has the effect of decreasing its size. These specially built pistons are designed so there is no interference with valves opening and closing.

This method solves a lot of problems, but . . . pistons are expensive. You'll find the prices starting at $8 at least and going up from there. You don't have to be a mathematical wizard to figure out that this initial outlay, plus new rings and gaskets, is going to blow the best part of a hundred dollars.

Figuring the Cost of Horses

Fixing up an old car is not an inexpensive hobby. Still, it is cheaper than rolling out a super edition of the latest Detroit creation. Also, once you've driven a brand new car around the block its value automatically drops by 25 percent. The first year's depreciation on an automobile is staggering. I've bought new cars for transportation since the pressure of work prevented me from tinkering with engines. I trade every three years and have about 45,000 miles on the car. Subtracting the trade-in from what I bought it for, I find that it cost me somewhere around $600 a year to drive these cars without figuring gas, oil, and normal maintenance.

You can pay $300 for a good used car. Then you can tack on another three for street-rodding it. You'll still be better off then I am moneywise with my new job, even though we theoretically spend the same amount of money for one year's driving. In fact, simple arithmetic shows that you can put $600 into your three-hundred-dollar job and come off better than I did financially if you keep the car for at least two years.

Besides that, you can have the exact car you want. Your souped-up performance will be better. You can make it a lot safer. If you'll go in for some fancy, but not necessarily expensive, customizing, you'll turn more heads than I will with my stock Rambler. In three years it'll cost me $600 a year to drive. In the same number of years your customized hot rod will cost you $300 at this comparison.

In addition, if you do a good job of rodding and customizing, you should have a better car than you started with. This means you'll get part of that $900 back when you unload it. If it is a popular job, you might even get more. It has happened.

Meanwhile, my $600 has been chopped up into dividends for motor-company stockholders. I get nothing for my money except the use of the car, since this depreciation is over what I got for trade in.

I have arbitrarily used these figures because they compare with what I spend on a low-cost compact. However, you can build a very good hot rod for less than the $600-to-$900 dollar range I've talked about here. You should be able to get by on $350, but the more you put into it, the more you're going to get out of it.

Now let's get back to compression. There is a lot more to be said about this most important part of souping up a car.

5

MORE SQUEEZE

Still another way to put more squeeze on the fuel mixture is by boring. Boring means punching out the cylinder holes to a bigger size than stock.

Boring for More Horsepower

In this technique increased compression is a by-product. The main reason for enlarging the cylinder holes is to increase displacement—that is, to pack more fuel into them. What this does is increase torque rating. Torque is the twisting power of the crankshaft in this case. This is what makes the back wheels spin.

When you increase the efficiency of your carburetion and ignition, much of the improvement is in high-speed performance. The same is true when you go to hotter cams to open and close your valves. It is the jack-rabbit competition cars that benefit most. Torque-rating improvements are felt in the lower speed ranges and are blessings to the street rodder.

Boring is usually associated with stroking, which we will get around to in a later paragraph.

Boring is a professional job. It cannot be done in a shade-tree garage. It must be taken to a first-class machine shop specializing in this kind of work and done with care and precision. The term *punch out* that rodders use in speaking of this operation is just part of car chatter. You don't *punch* anything—you *grind*. Like the mills of the gods, you grind "slowly, yet exceeding small."

Boring, enlarging the cylinder holes, can give your mill more power, but it can also give you trouble unless it's done by a really first-rate machine shop.

If this boring is confined to the swept area of the cylinder and the combustion chamber is untouched, then the compression ratio will be changed. We will be packing more fuel into the same combustion space. The effect is the same as in milling, but achieved in a different manner. In milling the swept volume remains the same, but the volume of the combustion chamber is reduced.

Of course, boring, stroking, milling, and the use of high-compression pistons can all be combined. The problem is

64 ○ *Hot Rodding for Beginners*

to avoid overcompression, however. Too much squeeze is worse than not enough. It can cause blown head gaskets, fractured pistons, "tuliped" valves, and heaven knows what else.

"Tell them," said one experienced hot rodder, "to do a little careful figuring before they start cutting metal. You'd be surprised at the number of beginners who go too far. They end up frantically trying to find ways to reduce compression again after building it up."

Cylinder Displacement—How to Figure It

Figuring cylinder displacement is simple. You don't have to do any measuring as we had to do in figuring the volume of an irregular-shaped combustion chamber. Displacement is the volume of fuel that the piston will displace or move out of its way on its rise from bottom dead center to top dead center. The number of cubic inches of displacement in one cylinder multiplied by the number of cylinders gives the engine's "cubes."

Here is the formula:

$$D = .7854 \times B^2 \times S \times N$$

If that looks confusing, it will become clear with a little study. D is displacement, the thing we are trying to find. The constant .7854 is nothing but pi (π) divided by 4. You use this figure as it is regardless of the changes in the other formula figures. B^2 is the bore squared, or multiplied by itself. S is the stroke and N is the number of cylinders.

Let's work out the formula using the figures from a current engine. For easy figuring we'll pick the small Ford 302 V-8 engine found in the Mustang. It has a four-inch bore and a three-inch stroke, according to engine specifications.

Substituting in the formula we get:

$D = .7584 \times 16 \times 3 \times 8$, or the constant times the bore multiplied by itself ($4 \times 4 = 16$) times the 3-inch stroke times the eight cylinders.

Multiplying the constant by the square of the bore by the stroke, we get the displacement of a single cylinder as 37.6972 cubic inches. When this is multiplied by the number of cylinders (8), we get the cubic-inch displacement of the engine as 301.5986.

Ford called it "302," but let's now waste breath over .4096 cubic inch when we have over 300.

You don't have to figure the stock displacement, since that is provided in the manufacturer's specifications. Where you need the formula is to see how much more you can gain by throwing his specs out the window.

We'd like to know the gain for ⅛-inch overbore. Just how much to increase cylinder size is a ticklish question. So we had best leave it dangling until we can give it our complete attention. Here we are concerned with how to figure the difference.

One eighth of an inch is .125 in the decimal system. Adding this to the four-inch bore and reworking the formula, I get 320.61 cubes as the new displacement.

That is, if I have multiplied and subtracted and added right. I didn't realize in high school math class that I was really being taught to build hot rods. I wish I had paid more attention. I also wish I had enrolled—assuming they would have let me—in the girl's Home Economics class. Maybe I would have learned enough about sewing to customize my own upholstery. A pro job on that costs a mint.

Cubes and Horses

The difference between the stock 302 and the overbored 320 is 18 additional cubic inches of fuel in the mill. How does this translate into horses? This varies with the engine. Roughly you get from a half horse to almost a full nag for each cubic inch. The heirs of Mr. Henry Ford claim their big V-8 gives .720 of a horse for each cubic inch and .915 for each cube in their 427 V-8. The gentlemen whose cars bear famed racer Louis Chevrolet's name claim .995 horse for each cube in their V-8 327. And the Chrysler V-8 383 is rated at .875.

Therefore if we take an average of .850, which *is* about average, even my poor arithmetic gets 9.18 additional horses from that one eighth-inch increase in the bore.

That isn't all the increase, however, since boring is usually combined with stroking for still more cubes. But before we get to stroking, let's consider how much we can enlarge the bore. If you cut too much, you break through into the water jacket that surrounds the cylinders to keep them cool. Even if you don't actually make a hole, you can weaken the walls. Then it is but a matter of time until you either junk the engine or go to a lot of unnecessary expense welding in a sleeve.

The general opinion of those I have talked with is that you can safely go only ⅛ inch (.125). Beyond this you are entering where racing experts fear to tread.

This .125 limit is for late-model engines. On older models it is safe to go to an overbore of 3/16. Some go-for-broke enthusiasts have gone as far as ⅜-inch overbore. This is dangerous.

How Much Will It Take?

Older engines had much thicker metal around the cylinders and will take a bigger overbore—provided that they haven't been bored already. On these older engines it will be well to get out pencil and paper and do a little figuring.

Modern engines cannot take as much boring as the older mills simply because the slide-rule boys in the factories have stolen the hot rodders' tricks. Often in a particular model of engine the only major difference is that the bore is cast a little bigger. Since the same block is used, it means that Detroit is doing the same thing a hot rodder does when he had his block bored. Making the bore larger to begin with cuts down the amount of metal that you can tinker with later. For example, the Chrysler small V-8 was brought out in 1964 with 318 cubes. The bore was 3.91 and the horsepower was 230 at 4,400 rpms. This engine was simply an overbore from a previous 273-cube engine which gave 190 horses. Its bore was 3.625. Then in 1968 the bore was increased to 4.040. The compression was raised from 9.2 to 1 to 10.5 to 1 and a four-barrel carb was stuck on in place of the previous duals. This combination produced 275 horses at 5,000 rpm. All three versions had 3.31-inch strokes. Other manufacturers are doing the same thing. They are upping horsepower by casting bigger bores.

So on older engines you can still take the bore route, but on newer ones you may not be able to cut enough to make the expense worthwhile.

Once Again—The Cost

The actual cost of having a mill bored is not so much. Prices vary with areas, of course, but figure on paying from $3 to $5 per cylinder. Unfortunately, punching out the holes is only the beginning of the price tag. Unless your new bore will take a factory piston, you may find yourself paying as much as $10 each for oversize hole-pluggers. Even without using my fingers to count on, I can tell you that this means $80. Of course, if you were going to special high-compression pistons anyway, the cost has already been figured in the budget.

Again, the danger is in accidently raising the compression too high. If you are going whole hog, then it is better to bore first and then figure the add-ons one at a time before you jump in.

Stroking Is Another Way

Boring is usually associated with stroking. Stroking is altering the crankshaft so that the pistons drop lower. This increases displacement and increases the compression ratio —because the swept volume of the cylinder is increased while the combustion chamber remains the same.

To find out how much stroking will increase the swept volume, use the following formula, since the stroking increase varies directly with the changed length of stroke:

> Stock stroke is to Altered stroke
> as Stock displacement is to New displacement
> (or swept volume)

Assuming an original stroke of three inches which we wish to increase to 3.25 on a 320-cube mill, we get the following:

68 ○ Hot Rodding for Beginners

$$3:3.25 = 40 : ND$$

We use 40 which is the swept volume of one cylinder of the 320 cube engine.
Then

$$3ND = 3.25 \times 40$$

or

$$3ND = 130 \text{ or } ND = 43.3$$

This means that the quarter-inch stroke has increased the swept volume 3.3 cubes per cylinder, or 26.4 cubes for the eight. The displacement has risen from 320 stock to 346.4.

To figure the compression ratio from the above, take the new 346.4 swept volume and add to it the cubes in the combustion chamber. We have previously measured this volume. Say it is 4 cubic inches. Add this to the swept volume to get combined swept-combustion volume. Then divide by the combustion volume to get the ratio. Your equation will look like this:

$$346.5 + 4 = 350.4 \div 4 = 8.76$$

Your new compression ratio using only the quarter-inch stroker for this particular combination is now 8.76 to 1.

Of course you would have to figure in also the increase from boring and milling if either or both of these operations were done also.

Boring and Stroking vs. Swap

Why do we go to all this trouble? Well, boring and stroking gives a small engine the muscle displacement of a bigger engine. So you might ask why we don't just pull an engine swap? These have become so popular that swap kits are available for the best known engines.

"Because," an experienced hot rodder will tell you, "in an engine swap you get the big engine's *weight* along with its increased muscle. Boring and stroking gives us the big engine's displacement while keeping the little engine's weight.

The lighter the load, the more your horses can put into acceleration and speed. You aren't wasting power just pulling a lot of weight along. In hot rodding, acceleration is a major goal. In drag racing it's the only goal. Every bit of weight you can leave on the cutting-room floor helps in a game where champions are often decided by split seconds."

Stroking Kits and Their Use

The easiest way to stroke is to buy a kit. They don't come cheap. Prices vary with area and companies and continuing inflation. Figure on not less than $350, however. A good crankshaft alone runs around $150. To this must be added new pistons, rings, and rods. Kits are available for popular mills. If you have a car there is no kit for, then all you can do is call on a professional to do it for you. It is not something you can do on weekends in a lean-to garage.

Stroking means welding the outside of the crankshaft journals and then regrinding the journals to bring the crankpin centers down. A lowering of $\frac{1}{16}$ inch increases the stroke $\frac{1}{8}$ inch, since the crank will pull the piston down $\frac{1}{16}$ inch and shove it up $\frac{1}{16}$ inch higher on the up-stroke.

Something has to be done about this rise. You can't have your pistons hammering into the head. Nor do you want them popping the rings out of the barrel. The solution is pistons that have their pins a little higher up.

Some engines will take more stroking than others. One quarter-inch to a half-inch are the most common. Some Olds owners go as much as $\frac{5}{8}$ inch on mills cast in the 1950's and later.

Stroker kits come complete. Ansen's Automotive Engineering in Los Angeles has long been a leader in this field, stocking a wide range of kits for various models of Ford, Chrysler, GM, Studebaker, and even Packards.

These kits come complete with reground crankshaft, pistons, connecting rods, bearings, and rings. The pistons and rods are pin-fitted. All you have to do is slip them in the barrel and connect to the crankshaft journals. Rods and pistons have been prealigned.

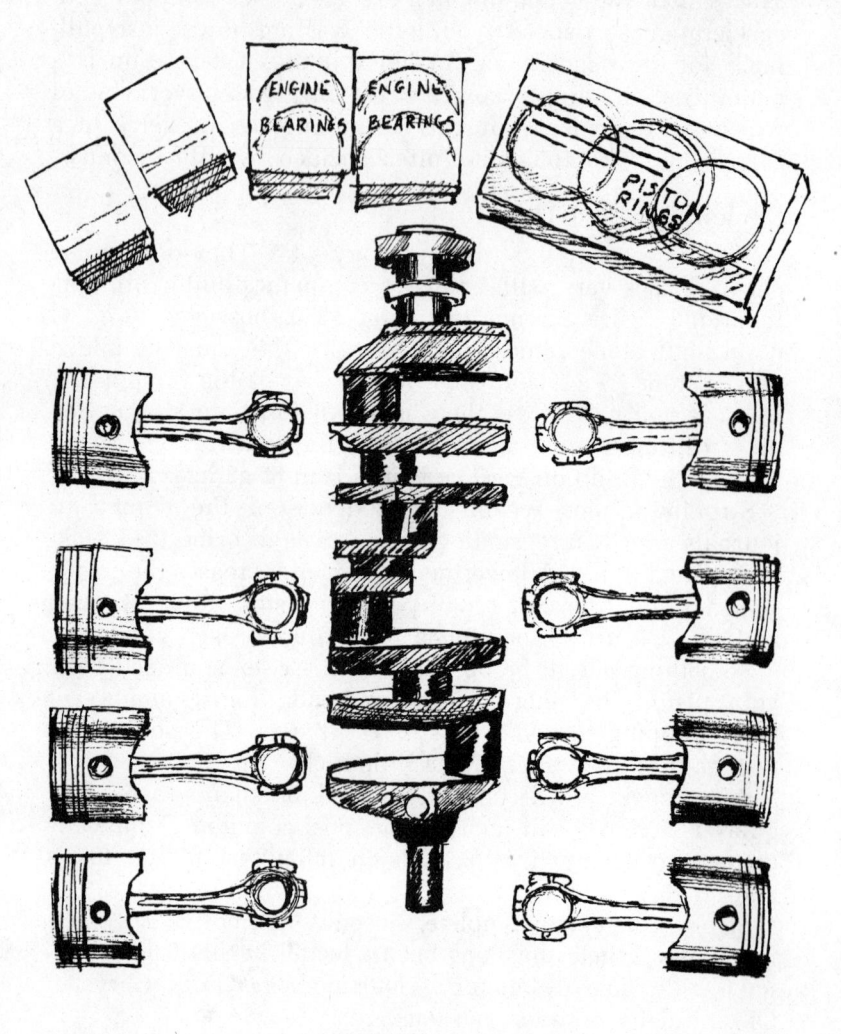

The easiest way to stroke is to buy a kit. Stroker kits come complete with reground crankshaft, pistons, connecting rods, bearings, and rings.

Problems of High Compression

Now when displacement and compression increase, they bring along a new problem. This is because the combined breathing apparatus—the carburetor, intake manifold, and intake valves—may not be able to supply enough fuel for the beefed-up demands of the larger cylinder bores.

Equally important is the problem of getting rid of the spent gases after their power has been transferred through the pistons to the crankshaft to become torque. This is thrown in just as a reminder that we haven't forgotten that an internal combustion engine has to breathe and exhale to live just as the human body. But before we get involved in breathing, let's finish up on the block while we have it stripped down for boring and stroking.

It is not sufficient just to bolt on high-speed goodies and hot-rodding gadgets. An engine is a team of parts all pulling in the same harness. Each part must do its share.

Maybe you remember James Russell Lowell's famous poem, "Wonderful One-Horse Shay." If not, then there's a lesson for hot rodders in its amusing rhymes. It's about a deacon who decides buggies failed because some part was weaker than the rest of the vehicle. So he constructed his one-horse shay with every part exactly as strong as the other.

So the shay drove and drove and drove. It lasted, I believe, exactly one hundred years and then one day collapsed into dust. Every part, which was just as strong as the other, wore out at once.

Blueprinting Your Engine

When hot rodders talk of "blueprinting" an engine they are trying to follow the deacon's lead. They go back to the manufacturer's specifications and bring the engine up to them, except where they are exceeded for souping purposes.

A lot of misguided souls seem to think that just because the spec writer in his air-conditioned office in Detroit put his figures on paper, cars come off the assembly line alike in all respects and parts and already "blueprinted," or made exactly to specifications. It ain't necessarily so, as the song goes. The whole idea of mass production is based on tolerances—the slight deviation from what the thoughtful engineer drew up is okay as long as it stays within certain limits. Blueprinting means tearing an engine down piece by piece and reassembling it the way it should have come out of the factory.

The idea is to make everything perfect. We are not exactly trying to follow in the deacon's footsteps, so there is no danger of a blueprinted mill falling to dust a hundred years from now. By the very nature of its work an automobile engine will wear certain parts faster than it will others. But what we are trying to do is to insure that each one does exactly the job it is supposed to do.

The first step is to get a list of specifications for your model. There shouldn't be any trouble doing this for cars made in the last 20 years. Check with dealers, garages, libraries, and back issues of hot-rodding magazines.

Times have changed, and many of the techniques used in the "old days" are obsolete now. However, old hot-rodding magazines still have many worthwhile material and pages of specifications on cars current when the magazines were published. I just picked up a stack that were 18 years old. They cost ten cents each.

Why You Work to Specs

Just exactly what you do depends upon your objective. If you have stock-car racing in mind, then you must stay within the stock limits specified by NASCAR for their sanctioned races or by whatever stock-car timing association rules you have to race under. Here you work to bring everything to spec. That means insuring that valve, piston, and ring clearances are exact. That valve springs are matched for tension. That each cylinder has exactly the swept volume it is supposed to have. That the combustion chamber is the size it is supposed to be. That the crankshaft is balanced. That the bores are straight—they don't taper ever so slightly. Take nothing on faith. Check it all and bring it up to spec.

Another thing to watch in these old engines is head warp. Lay a straightedge across the mating surface. If not exactly flat—possibly due to somebody not using a torque wrench in

It's smart to check an old engine for head warp. Lay a straightedge across the mating surface to see if it is perfectly flat.

tightening it down after an overhaul—then start hunting a milling machine.

In short, bring everything up to perfection except those items which we have chosen to go beyond spec—such as increased compression, stroking, porting, relieving, etc. (We'll discuss the last two items in the next chapter.)

In working on the block of an old engine it is very important to inspect it carefully. Look for tiny cracks in the metal around the cylinder bores. Especially check around the valve seats and around the spark-plug holes in the heads of flathead engines.

We have already mentioned insuring proper clearances. This is done to reduce friction and resulting overheating, and also to insure that oil circulates satisfactorily. This matter of oil circulation cannot be overemphasized. Many hot rodders groove their crankshaft main-bearing journals to insure sufficient lubrication for the tough workload they intend to put on the mill.

If you don't want to go this far, at least thoroughly clean every oil hole and groove.

6

TAKE A DEEP BREATH

Milling, boring, and stroking—with their added displacement and increased compression—*could* add more horses to your automotive team.

We say *could,* because a bigger hole to pack more fuel into won't help any unless more fuel can get in. The system bolted on in Detroit for the smaller cubes may not be enough to feed a hopped-up mill. In this case all your work and expense have only succeeded in reducing rather than increasing performance. So our next important step is to insure that the mill can take a good deep breath each time the valve ports open.

This means that fuel, fuel pump, carburetor, intake manifold, camshaft, and valves must all be brought into a smooth working team. Then if their efficiency peaks right with the efficiency of our reworked cylinders, we're finally in business. Provided, of course that we don't forget to blueprint the ignition system along with the other two hot-rodding essentials.

Ignition is a topic for later in the day. Right now we are concerned with getting the proper fuel mixture into the cylinders and getting the burned gases out.

Getting the Fuel In

First, let's take a quick review of an automobile fuel system. It starts with the stuff in the tank. This combustible material is fed by a fuel pump into a carburetor. A carburetor is nothing but a metering device that shoots a stream of the liquid fuel into a fast-moving stream of air. The fuel mixes with the air in a vapor that will burn properly inside the engine. This vapor is collected into an intake manifold. From here it is drawn through the open valves into the cylinders during the intake stroke. The compression stroke gives it a squeeze and the ignition system sets it afire. The heated gas expands rapidly, pushing down the piston for the power stroke, which is where the muscle lies. Then the piston, returning for the exhaust stroke, pushes the burned gases out the exhaust ports.

All this is a very simple process, but getting everything to work right is not so simple. On a stock car the problems have been slide-ruled by the Detroit deacons who keep trying to build a wonderful one-horse shay that will satisfy everybody. Since they can't, our changes in the block will require corresponding changes throughout the fuel system.

Fuels Other Than Gasoline

Let's start with the fuel. We'll assume that you'll begin with gasoline—that standby which has served the automobile from the horseless carriage to the many-horsed chariot.

The first thing a beginner starts asking is about the super-soups he reads about the pros using. So we might as well throw in a word about them.

The first word is a warning. These "hot" fuels are hot to handle. For a beginner they are too hot to handle. These fuels pack more wallop and give horsepower increases of at least 10 percent and usually much more over regular gasoline. For drag racing where runs are timed in seconds, it is possible to squeeze out much higher increases.

Now if we have been boring and stroking and milling and praying for increased horsepower all along, then why must we be so wary of what seems the simplest way of getting it —pouring it into the gas tank?

We will not have to fumble for an answer. It is simply that we look on a car as we look on the sun. We'd like to peek out the window tomorrow morning and still see it there where it is supposed to be. A lot of time and money, not to speak of love, goes into souping up these cars. It is no fun having to sweep up the parts in a dust pan. And that is what can happen if you don't know exactly what you are doing with hot fuels.

Also, they are too hot for anything but all-out competition driving. If you must drive your heap on the street, to school, to work or to take Susie to the drive-in movie, don't waste time dreaming about super-soups.

About the cheapest nitro fuel you can pick up has a price tag of $4.50 a gallon. And for special exotic mixtures it can go up and *up*. You don't have to be much of a mathematician to figure that just ten gallons of that stuff is going to blow a $50 bill.

Since the carburetor jet sizes must be enlarged for these fuels, it is not practical to switch back and forth. Also, some of the hot fuels, notably nitrobenzene, are toxic. Breathe its fumes and *your* light goes out.

These nitro fuels are corrosive. They really mess up aluminum and form explosive salts with copper and lead. They can't be left standing around in the fuel tank. Flushing out the lines after use is a standard procedure. Use alcohol for the flushing.

This is not to say that there isn't a place for these nitro super-soups. But that place is in all-out competition machines that will be babied and pulled to the strips and tracks. Preignition is more disastrous here than when one uses gasoline. Not only does all roughness have to be polished out of the combustion chambers, but they should be cleaned after every race. Otherwise bits of carbon can cause preignition.

These nitro fuels—nitromethane, nitroethene, and nitrobenzene—are most commonly mixed with methyl alcohol (methanol) for use. Users have their favorite formulas and proportions.

Gasoline Vapor and Air

We'll leave the nitros until we gain experience, settling on gasoline. If we have upped compression, this will have to be premium high octane to prevent preignition. This gas is pumped into the carburetor bowl, where its level is regu-

78 ○ **Hot Rodding for Beginners**

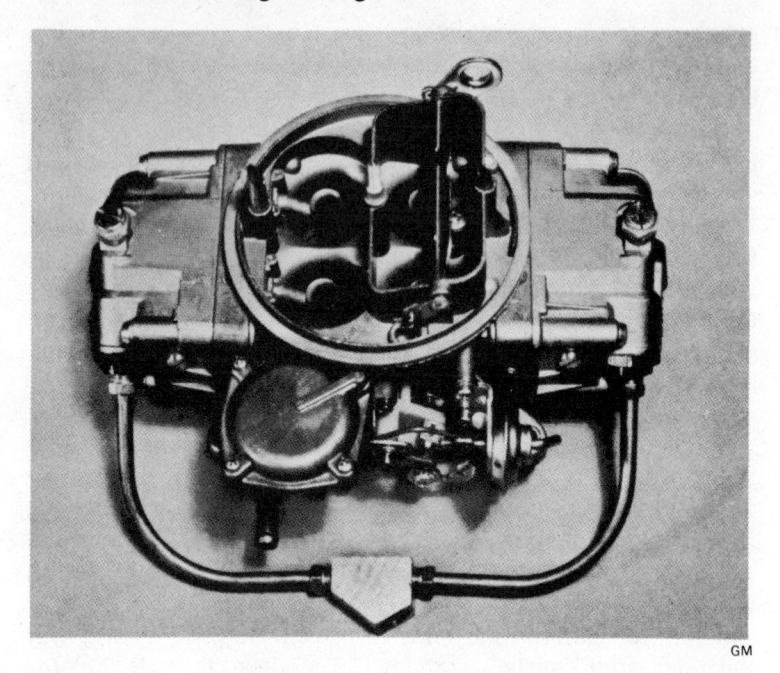

This is a typical 4-barrel carburetor that is stock equipment on some Detroit high-performance powerplants.

lated by a float which adjusts the flow of gas through a needle valve. A jet leads from this bowl into the carburetor's air stream.

This air stream is a *venturi*. A venturi (named after the Italian physicist G. B. Venturi) resembles a rocket nozzle. Take a piece of pipe and squeeze it in the middle so that this throat is narrower than either end. The result is a venturi. If any kind of fluid—and air is a fluid—is rushed through such a constricted pipe, its speed will increase while going through the narrow throat. As the speed increases, the air pressure drops. Since the air pressure in the venturi throat is now less than the air pressure in the float bowl, the speeding air sucks fuel up through the jet into the air stream.

The mixture—now vaporized—passes into the intake manifold. It is necessary to vaporize the fuel because liquid gasoline will not burn. Okay, so you know a guy who used a match to check the gasoline in his tank and he hasn't come down yet. It was not the liquid gas that exploded. He ignited the fumes off the gas.

Oxygen in the air is necessary to support combustion of our gas. Without air the stuff won't burn. It won't burn either if there is too little gas mixed with the air (lean mixture) or too much gas mixed with it (rich mixture).

There must be at least one part of gasoline to sixteen parts of air before the mixture will burn. If there is any less gas the mixture is too lean to burn. The mixture will continue to burn until the ratio of air to gas passes eight parts of air to one of gasoline. Then the mixture is too rich to burn. The best mixture for power is somewhere midway between these lean and rich extremes.

If you are running too rich a mixture, you'll see black smoke from the exhaust and feel a power loss. If too lean, you lose power from engine starvation. Worse yet, a too-lean gas/air mix burns slower. This may lead to backfiring. This happens because there may still be burning gas in the cylinder when the intake valve opens to let in fresh fuel. It may ignite and shoot fire through the manifold and into the carburetor.

Carburetion—All Kinds

Adjusting the carburetor mixture is a simple part of tune-up. At the same time you should inspect all gaskets. The carb needle valve should be checked along with the float. Clean all passages with blasts of compressed air. Linkages should be checked and the automatic choke—if you have one—should be cleaned.

This is about all that needs to be done to a mildly souped-up street car. But if you've gone in for boring, stroking, and milling, then that single carb may not be enough to fill your larger cylinders. You may have to go the multiple-carb route. This will not only require bolting on new carburetors, but will also require new manifolds.

On a single carburetor setup, the fuel mixture enters the manifold at the center, spreading out to fill the manifold until an opening intake valve permits some of the mixture to be sucked into the cylinder. This means that the mixture will be richer in the center of the manifold and leaner at each end.

This difference is not great, but it is sufficient to make performance lower than it should be. For normal, everyday street driving it is plenty good enough, but for all-out performance a better distribution of fuel in the manifold is essential.

Early hot rodders solved the problem by going to dual carbs with the two linked together. Delighted drivers reported that they picked up ten extra horses this way. So if two were so good, then why not go for three? They did, and the combination gave as much as 25 extra horsepower.

Unfortunately every Eden has its snake. The three carb setup was great at high speed, but when society demands you slow up on its streets, the three carbs overloaded the manifold. The mills ran rough and the gasoline waste was enough to break the bank.

Multiple Carburation and Linkages

Troubles, frustrations, and roadblocks are meat to a genuine hot rodder. They ate up this roadblock. The answer was progressive linkage. Kits are available, so it is a simple bolt-on deal. The linkage is so arranged that depressing the throttle opens up the center carburetor only. This feeds the mill through the lower speed ranges. Then at the point where you want it, the two secondary carbs cut in.

This is done with simple ingenuity. The first and third carbs' throttle arms are linked together by a small rod that bypasses the center primary carburetor. Then another rod links the first carb to the primary. However, this is a sliding bolt which slips through the junction with the first secondary carburetor so that its throttle arm is not moved until it strikes a set nut when the primary carb is already half open.

What this does is to permit the mill to run on the primary carb only at low speeds where the other two are not needed.

Then all the driver has to do is push the foot throttle past the halfway mark and the secondary pots go into action, providing the extra push now that they are needed.

Multiple carburetion requires special manifolds to hold the extra pots. These can be bought in a variety of sizes for anything from a simple dual setup to expensive and elaborate arrangements that provide a carburetor for each cylinder.

Such elaborate setups are for competition vehicles. They are too hot for street rods. If you are working on a street rod and need dual carbs to feed your increased displacement, the cheapest out on older cars is to get a Y adapter, which will permit you to set two pots over the single manifold port. It is not as efficient, of course, as putting on a carefully designed manifold made for dual carburetion. The fuel passages won't pass the mixture as well as the special job.

Nonprogressive Linkage

We are talking here about older engines, of course, and those that will be used for both street and mild competition. For all-out dragging where you have to have full power from the word go or you're an also-ran, progressive linkage is out. When you drop the clutch, you want everything you can squeeze out of your horses. In this case, what you need is a nonprogressive linkage. The carbs are tied together so they open simultaneously whether you have two or eight.

If you go this route, there should be no installation problems. You close the butterfly valves in the carbs and then link the throttle arms so they open together. Just make sure that there is no binding anywhere.

In 1954 Detroit climbed on the multiple-carburetor bandwagon with their "quads." A quad is four single-throat carbs built into a single carburetor body and works the same way as multiple single pots. Two of the throats are primaries and two are secondaries. There is a built-in progressive linkage. This uses the primaries for lower speeds and then kicks in the secondaries when increased speed calls for more juice. Some use air-pressure principles to bring in the secondaries, but the principle is the same.

Arrow points to the connecting bar hooking together the twin quad carbs on this beautifully chromed show engine.

Manifolds for Multiple Carburetion

These multiple-carburetor systems require special manifolds. A single-throat carburetor—and you'll only find them today on the smaller compact cars—must feed all the cylinders and calls for a manifold that will distribute the fuel mixture as best it can to all of them. The dual-carb manifold splits the job, with each throat feeding half the cylinders.

They don't split right down the middle with one throat

feeding one bank and the other throat feeding the opposite bank in the V-8 engine. The manifold is built so that one throat feeds the two inner cylinders of both banks and the other handles the outer two on both banks. This division is based upon the mill's firing order.

The reason for this arrangement is so that intake impulses of fuel through the throats will be alternately spaced between the two banks of cylinders. Otherwise you would have two or more impulses at the same time and then delays. This way there is a more even flow.

An exception to this is the "log" manifolds which you often see on competition cars, but which are too hot for street jobs. The log manifold serves an entire bank, but supports two or more carbs for each. The interior is modified to equalize the fuel mixture between cylinders.

Carburetor Adjustments and Remodeling

Carburetors are basically simple and are not difficult to work on. They all work on the same principle, and there are but a few basic models. However—and this is important to remember—a basic model will vary according to the mill it was originally designed for.

I recall one beginner who couldn't understand why a Carter AFB (the initials stand for *aluminum four-barrel*) he picked up in a wrecking yard couldn't be bolted right on his own heap in place of a Carter AFB he was taking off.

The answer is simple enough. While the two look the same on the outside, there are often internal differences needed to modify the basic carb to fit a particular engine. For one thing, even if they look the same inside, you will find the sizes of the metering jets and rods varying considerably in size. Also the venturi will probably vary in size also.

Then too there is the possibility that the carb has been modified by some owner who changed jet sizes after modifying the engine.

The stock jets in a carburetor are designed for normal cruising. They are intended for the twin purpose of smooth running at these speeds and for reasonable fuel economy. Assuming that you have torn down the carb, cleaned it (boiling it out, as mechanics say), adjusted the parts to required tolerances, checked the needle valve for proper seating, assuring that the float maintains the proper fuel level and that there is no binding—then the only thing left to do is adjust the idle setscrew to the best performance at the desired idle rpm's (revolutions per minute).

If there is access to a chassis dynamometer, then you can get an accurate check on the air-fuel mixture. Otherwise, all you can do is set the idle mixture by the "hear and feel" method. You tighten it down until the engine almost stops and then back off until it sounds just right.

This adjustment is for the low-speed metering system. This does not drive the car at high speeds. The main metering jet requires a stronger pull to drag the gas out into the venturi air stream. Therefore until the crankshaft reaches the proper speed, it does not come into action.

A road test can give an indication of how well the air-fuel mixture is set for your car. If too lean, operation may be a little like running the car on a cold morning without proper choke. There may be surging and backfire on acceleration. If too rich, the response may be mushy when you tromp on the throttle.

Once carbs had adjustments to permit changing the air-fuel mixture to accommodate different mixture ratios. Modern carburetors have only the idle adjustment. You change the air-fuel mixture by changing the jets or jet and metering-rod assemblies. Take the next size leaner jet or metering rod, or the next size richer—and work up from there.

As a general rule, competition cars require richer mixtures than street rods. Stock-car racers usually want a slightly richer mixture than drag racers.

Checking Out Your Carb or Carbs

If acceleration is what you are after, then the drag strip is your proving ground.

"Start off by clocking your e.t. (elapsed time) and speed with the stock jets," one dragster informs us. "Then repeat with the next richer jetting. If things get better, you are going in the right direction. Try the next richer jet and keep going until things get worse. Then back off."

Multiple-carburetor systems may give the beginner a bit of a problem in adjusting the idle. In single-throat carbs it is simply a matter of twisting the idle adjusting screw until the flow of fuel is correct for the amount of air coming through the venturi.

Multiple carbs may demand that you adjust the air flow as well. Lately gauges have been put on the market that help. These are slipped over the air-intake to register the air flow. The throttle valve is then adjusted so that each throat is passing the same amount of air. Then the idle adjusting screw is set so that each gets the same amount of fuel.

This is important for street rods where you step off from idle. In competition driving where you start with the throttle wide open, there is no point in worrying about how the low-speed jets operate.

Keep It Clean

All this business of worrying about just the right size carb jets is wasted time if you don't keep the carburetor clean. A dirty "jug" can undo all your work. Clogged filters or dirt in the line can restrict the flow of fuel to the carb. Loose connections may permit air to be sucked into the line which can stop the flow of fuel entirely. Gum in the carburetor's idle jet can cause rough idling.

The need for cleanliness makes the carburetor air cleaner about as important a part of the car as you can find. The quickest way to foul up a carb is to let dirt get sucked in with the air. Ask some of the boys who raced on dirt tracks before the paper-filter air cleaner was devised. Often they were lucky to finish a race without a carburetor cutting out on them.

Paper-filter cleaner elements are made of porous paper that lets the air through, but which can stop the smallest particles of grit. They are entirely efficient if kept clean and replaced when necessary.

Previous types, which employed an oil-wetted mesh and

an oil bath, are obsolete. You may still find them on older models. The best thing to do with them is to dig a deep hole and bury them.

Regardless of the type of filter used, it must be kept clean. Otherwise it can become so clogged with dirt that it restricts the flow of air into the carburetor. You might just as well run with the choke out as with a clogged air filter.

Oil-wetted and oil-bath filters must be washed out with solvent and reoiled. Paper types are simpler. The pleated paper filter is removed from the air-cleaner housing. Loose dirt is knocked out by tapping it against the top of the work table. If this doesn't clean it and if dirt is embedded in the paper, replace the filter.

Superchargers

Among the first questions beginning hot rodders ask is about superchargers—called blowers—and fuel injection. Both of these are definitely in the post-graduate class.

What the supercharger does is to compress the intake air, putting an increased weight of air into a smaller volume. This means that the increased weight of air can carry increased amounts of fuel. In effect the supercharger increases an engines compression. If you have already done this by boring, stroking, or milling, you can't use a supercharger. It'll run the compression so high you may find yourself picking up the engine in pieces.

If a supercharger will effectively increase compression, why not use it instead of going the boring and stroking route? For one thing, something has to furnish the power to pull your blower. It doesn't run itself. That power comes from your engine. Do you remember way back when we said that the boys in Detroit like to rate their engines in gross horsepower? This is the rated horsepower of a bare engine, pulling nothing but its own internal working parts. Now everything added to that engine takes some of that horsepower to do its own work. What is left is called *net horsepower*. You have to figure out if what you are going to get out of the blower will offset the horsepower it costs you to run it.

There is no question but that supercharging can make some dramatic increases in horsepower. On top-competition vehicles they are now standard. A driver would as soon go on the track without his pants as without his blower. He'd just naturally feel undressed.

Generally a beginner must content himself with stock-car and street-rod competition. In many classes of competition superchargers are out.

Then there is the price. A good blower will cost somewhere around $250. Add this to the cost of fuel injection and we're talking in the range of $550 to $600 total—which is more than we figure on a beginner budgeting for a hot rod.

Fuel-Injection Systems

Fuel injection dispenses with the carburetor entirely. It is a system of carefully metering an exact amount of fuel into each cylinder. Originally designed for racing cars, fuel injection has become the darling of hot rodders as well.

Hilborn is the pioneer who blazed the trail for the average hot rodder, manufacturing fuel-injection systems for most of the popular models. The Hilborn is made by the Fuel Injection Engineering Company, Santa Monica, California.

Fuel injection is controversial among hot rodders. You can get some loud arguments on the pros and cons of FI versus carbs. Since fuel injection is, along with nitro fuels, something for the expert to tinker with, we'll not go into these arguments here.

Before we get off the subject of engine breathing, we should say a word or two about porting and polishing. There was a time when porting was one of the most important steps in souping up a mill. Now that Detroit has started catching up with us, you don't see much of it anymore. However, since beginners often pick older cars to build up, you might run into a mill that demands the old technique.

On these older engines the intake ports were too small to adequately feed the cylinders after they were enlarged by boring and stroking. Then they were enlarged by grinding away metal. Today Detroit has enlarged them about as far as you can go. So there is no more metal to cut. On such engines about all you can do is to polish the ports. This means smoothing them down to remove any rough places so the air-fuel mixture will flow more smoothly. You remove only enough metal to smooth things out.

In fact, enlarging ports slows down the velocity of the mixture. This made no difference in the mill that has been bored and stroked, since the added pull of the larger bore offset the velocity drop caused by the enlarged port.

Valves, Camshafts, and Balancing

While you are polishing, move on up into the combustion chamber. Here any roughness is an invitation for carbon to hang on it. Then the carbon's afterglow is a sure route to preignition.

Now we are ready to start on the valves. First begin with a careful check. If the valves do not seat properly, a valve grind may be indicated. Check the valve lifters for any drag. Are the valves burned? Are the valve stems straight? Do they all have the same length? Check the valve springs.

If the head has been milled, then check to see that there is sufficient clearance for the valves to open. The usual recommendation here is to use strips of children's molding clay. Press it on the top of the combustion chamber just above the valves. Screw the head down and turn over the engine several times.

Now take off the head again and take a look at the clay to see how far the valves pressed into the strips. There must be at least 0.060 inch clearance. If there isn't, then get out the grinder and start cutting. But remember, if you do, that this will change the compression ratio again.

On overhead valve mills, pistons are available with cuts in the head to give additional valve clearances when needed.

We also should give a thought to balancing the valves. Big balance jobs like crankshafts, clutches, and flywheels require electronic balancing and are jobs for the pro shop. On valves you can get by with a small pair of postal scales. You weight each one and grind them down slightly to matched weights. They are supposed to come off the assembly line as alike as two peas in the proverbial pod, but they never do.

This slight difference in weight may seem a small matter, but out-of-balance assemblies not only eat into your horsepower, they also are subject to greater wear. You don't notice it since they are hidden inside, but take a look at a tire that is run on an unbalanced wheel and you will get an idea what can happen. The importance of balancing an engine's moving parts should not be overlooked. All your major efforts and expense in mill souping can be cut back because you ignore a few of the smaller items.

Now to get back to valves—the heart of their action lies in the camshafts that activate them. This is a really hot item with hot rodders. We'll see why in the next chapter.

7

CAMS, SPARK, AND EXHAUST

Cams are a hot item—both for the car and for hot-rodding arguments. No two builders or grinders agree exactly on what is best. Mainly, however, it is a matter of what you are after.

The camshaft, to review briefly, draws its power via a timing chain and gear from the crankshaft. It is covered with nodes or cams which raise and lower the valves as the camshaft revolves. A hotter cam does not add to torque in itself. However, it does determine when the valves open, how long they stay open, and how quickly they close. This, in turn, has a powerful effect upon whether the mill generates all the torque it is capable of putting out.

Cams and Tappets—How They Work

A cam can roughly be compared to a pear. The bottom is a regular part of a circle, but the upper part bulges out from the bottom in a distinct pear shape. The valve lifters (or tappets), which are sliding rods, rest against this cam. When the bottom of the cam is on top, the valves are closed. But as the camshaft turns, the tappets ride upward along the bulging surface of the cam. This pushes the tappets —valve lifters, pushrods, or whatever they call them in your locality—upward. This in turn tips the rocker arms so they press downward on the overhead valve stems. The valves open. Then after the cam passes its peak, the tappets ride down and the valves are closed by the valve springs.

Now the *shape* of this bulge or off-center section determines what happens. If the rise is a gentle slope, then the valve opening will be more gradual than if the rise is sharp. Generally cams are reground to different contours to give a higher valve lift and to provide a longer period for the valves to stay open.

When dealing with stock cams, we are again faced with the "average" problem which keeps stock cars from being top performers. The cams on these cars were ground to give best performance at street-driving speeds. While they are much hotter than they used to be, they still starve an engine at top speeds. This is because the valves open and close so fast that sufficient fuel cannot be drawn into the cylinders. The situation is made even worse if the mill has been bored and stroked, since there are additional cubes to pack full of fuel.

The solution would seem to be to increase the time that the valves remain open. This is what a reground "hot" cam does. Unfortunately, improving the speed performance in this manner causes low-speed performance to suffer. What happens is that intake time and exhaust time start to overlap, with a resulting loss in compression.

Cam Grinding—When to Do It

In some grinds the intake valve is still open when the compression stroke begins. At low speeds this can force some of the fuel mixture back out of the cylinder before the valve closes. The resulting performance becomes so bad that the car cannot run satisfactorily. However, when the speed picks up, the valves open and close so fast that the overlap is no longer the problem it is at slower speeds. This is why racing cars rev up so high in starting. Starting at high rpm ranges requires transmission ratios that will stand the shock.

The point at which overlap ceases to be a problem is known as the *cut-in speed*. When this happens it is much like when a pilot cuts in the afterburner on his jet. You can feel the renewed surge of power.

Nothing can be done to grind a cam so that it is capable

of top performance at both high and low speed ranges. So if your car must run on the streets, you can't put in one of the hotter cams. You have to decide what you'll use the car for, then stick with a cam ground for that purpose. Custom cam grinders have just about covered the field. There is a camshaft or camshaft kit for every purpose. Just remember that each separate grind was designed for a specific purpose. Use it for that purpose and it will serve you well. If you don't use it for the speed range it was designed for, then you have wasted your money.

Buying the Right Cam

The first step above the stock cam is the semi-race cam. It gives good acceleration and idles smoothly, but gives only a small increase in top speed.

For still further increase in top performance, the next change is to the ¾ grind. If yours is one of the older mills, this may be as far as you can go on a car that must fight street traffic. Idling will be rougher, but top speed improves and acceleration takes a sizable jump for the better.

If you try to go any higher with a street rod, you have to rev up too high to keep the mill percolating when you are idling. Then when you take your foot off the clutch, your next operation is to pull your front end out of the back end of the slower car in front of you.

Generally when sticking a ¾-race cam in an older car, you have to up the compression ratio and give some thought to increasing carburetion, if you haven't already done so. The three go hand in hand. Also, if the mill is going to turn faster, then you have to get the exhaust out faster, which means a minimum of two exhaust pipes. We'll discuss this in more detail later.

One word of caution, however. There is no standard for cam regrinding. Each manufacturer has his own ideas and methods for working out those ideas. Consequently what one calls a ¾ race may not give the same performance in your mill that a ¾ race from another grinder will. This does not mean that either one of them is wrong. Each designed the

Cams, Spark, and Exhaust ○ 93

recontouring for a specific purpose and often with a specific model of engine in mind. The size of the valves, length of the pushrods, arrangement of the rocker arms, and other factors all must be considered. So it is best to stick with grinds made especially for your particular model.

At least, it is best to do so in the beginning. Later as you gain experience it is safe to experiment—provided, of course, that you are in a financial position to be wrong and start over again.

Hot, Hotter, Hottest

The next step up is directly into the competition class and is known as full-race. Don't let the name fool you. There are hotter cams than full-race. This name is a hangover from the old days.

These hotter cams cannot be bought and bolted in. They won't run in a stock engine. You must have a minimum of 9.25-to-1 compression ratio and multiple carburetion. Porting may be indicated in older engines. If not, then the ports should at least be polished. Hotter ignitions are necessary and more care must be taken to insure an adequate exhaust.

The super-grinds beyond full-race demand extreme compression ratios and are useless at revolutions below 2,500 rpm. Cubes have to be increased, and fuel injection or multiple carburetion added.

Cams for regrinding are either new stock cams or old ones taken by cam grinders in trade. They are reground on automatic cam-grinding machinery which follows a template made to the exact shape of the desired finished camshaft. This is okay for mild regrinding, but if the cut is radical it will lead to fast wearout.

The trouble is that camshafts are hardened on the outer surface and left comparatively soft on the inside. Swordmakers used to temper their blades the same way. They claimed that if the metal was hardened equally all the way through, the resulting blade was more brittle.

Too radical a grind can wear away this hard outer surface and leave the softer metal to take the beating from the tappets. Some grinders claim they retemper after grinding. Others claim to use a differently hardened steel stock.

In any event, buying a cam is not a hit-and-miss affair. You should explain exactly what you want it to do to the speed-shop clerk. Then be guided by his advice. It cannot be overemphasized that no cam grind can cover all performance ranges. You need a different grind for a street job than for a dragster and one different from both of these for stock-car racing.

Because of these differences in cams, it is not a good idea to try and make do with your old tappets and pushrods. Most cam grinders will sell you a complete kit in which the individual items are made and balanced to work with each other. Sometimes—but not always—these kits also include new valve springs. This is good, for you generally need stronger springs when going to hotter cams.

Removing and Replacement of Cams

Removing and replacing a cam is simple enough. You can easily do the job yourself with a little help from the technical manual for the model you own.

Occasionally it is possible to pull the radiator and replace the camshaft without pulling the engine. Otherwise the mill will have to be taken out. You begin by removing the fan and fan pulley. Next you take off the timing-chain cover, the cam-timing gear (it is the larger of the two under the cover), and the timing chain. Next remove the pushrods and tappets. Now the cam can be slid out. The new cam is then slid *gently* into the block. Be careful not to damage the lobes.

These are general instructions only to show how simple the procedure is. Each cam kit comes complete with installation instructions. Follow them religiously. They were written by people who know exactly what they are doing and who are interested in your getting the best service from their products.

Once the cam is in place, it must be timed. The cam lobes must work in harmony with the crankshaft so that they open the valves at the right time during the right cylinder cycle.

Valve timing is done by lining up timing marks on the

Cams, Spark, and Exhaust ○ 95

crankshaft sprocket and the camshaft sprocket. Use a straight-edge across the center of the crankshaft and the camshaft, lining up the marks with it. Then place the timing-gear chain in place over the sprockets.

Getting Rid of the Exhaust

In replacing the valve-chain cover, be sure to pay particular attention to the oil seal.

Cams are concerned with getting fuel into the engine. It is equally important to get it out. Detroit's stock exhausts do not do the job as it should be done.

The trouble is that collector pipes are too small and the

Getting the exhaust out of an engine is as important as getting gas in. These dramatic-looking collector pipes give an unusual appearance to this "vintage tin" Model T.

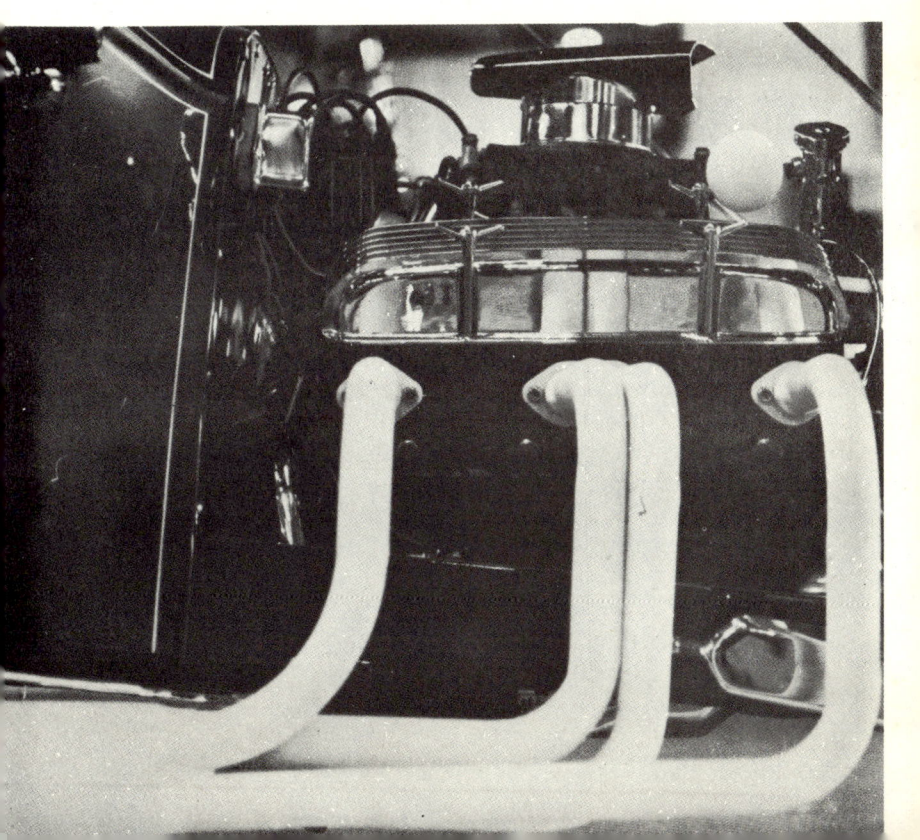

noise-stifling mufflers create back pressure. Exhaust gases can't get out fast enough and they pile up in the manifold. This means that when the exhaust valves open there is no free flow of waste gases out of the cylinders. Of course, the up-stroke of the piston forces it out, but then pressure in the exhaust manifold forces some back in before the exhaust valves can close. These unexpelled exhaust gases dilute the incoming fuel mixture. This robs the engine of part of its power.

Some late-model cars come with dual-exhaust systems designed to correct this trouble. Generally they still are not adequate for a souped up engine. The fault here may lie not in the twin-exhaust system itself, but in the exhaust manifolds. Exhaust gas must have a free, unrestricted passageway to get itself out and away from the exhaust valves. Unfortunately, design considerations do not always permit a manufacturer to give as much space to the exhaust manifold as he would like. And, of course, mass production is an enemy of precision.

Headers

Stock exhaust systems on cars manufactured within the last 15 years are usually adequate for street rods, but you can still pick up a few extra horses by going the header route. Headers are officially known as "collection systems for removing exhaust gases." All of which means that they are a cleaner-flowing design of exhaust.

Exhaust systems come in all shapes and designs. Some wind around in a maze of pipes. Others stick a multitude of pipes into the air. Still another will feature "zoomies"—pipes that point down and outward in front of the rear tires. A lot of these curious designs may be more for show than for practical use. However, if the individual pipes are gathered into a single pipe, a suction is created that helps pull the exhaust out.

Mufflers

A muffler, even the best of the low-pressure type, is a genuine horse thief. For street jobs there is nothing you can

Cams, Spark, and Exhaust ○ 97

do about it. You must keep your heap quiet enough to avoid telling it to the judge. You get the lowest-pressure muffler you can to minimize the back pressure as much as possible.

On the drag strips, mufflers are as popular as a Chevvy salesman at a Ford convention, but are required on many classes. The National Hot Rod Association rules for the stock-car division permits dual exhausts and headers, but insists that the exhaust be routed through a muffler and tail pipe. "Open bypasses may be used, but must be installed in front of the muffler," the rules say. A bypass is a valve that can be opened ahead of the muffler to let the exhaust escape before it hits the muffler.

The same requirement prevails for the Modified Production Section, but higher-performance classes ask only that the system you use terminate in a collector permanently attached to your car.

More About Ignition

Now that we have gotten the fuel into the cylinders and out again, it is time to backtrack a bit and pick up the problems of making the mixture burn in the first place. This is the job of the ignition, the last member of the team we must consider in getting maximum performance from the mill.

To briefly review what we said earlier about the ignition system, it all begins with the battery. The current flows from the battery to the coil where the low battery voltage is stepped up to high voltage. This is done by creating a magnetic field from current flowing through the primary winding inside the coil. When this primary circuit is broken by the opening of the contact points inside the distributor, the magnetic field collapses. The secondary windings in the coil are induced to gather a stepped-up current by the collapsing magnetic field. This secondary voltage may be as high as 25,000 volts. This voltage goes into the distributor which, by means of a rotating rotor, is distributed to each spark plug just prior to top dead center of the compression stroke.

This is the way we described it in our original discussion of the car's cycle of operation, and this applies to the 6-volt

98 ○ Hot Rodding for Beginners

system. If the car has a 12-volt system, there will also be included in the circuit an ignition resistor. This reduces the voltage applied to the coil and points during the operation of the car. This resistor is cut out when the car is cranked so that the starter—which requires all the juice it can get—can get the full 12-volt charge.

The problem is that in a speeding car there is only $\frac{1}{300}$ of a second or less for the ignition to build up a magnetic field, collapse it by breaking the ignition points, induce the high voltage in the secondary coil, and flash the built-up charge to the distributor, then to the spark plugs.

Ignition systems are built to handle the workload of a stock car. When we start souping, the system may not be good enough to handle the increased performance we have now built into the mill. When the compression of the engine is increased, the fuel mixture is more tightly packed in the cylinder. This heavier mixture acts as a resistor to the spark, which must jump between the electrodes of the spark plug in order to ignite the fuel. It is harder for the spark to make the jump when compression is increased.

Getting a Stronger Spark

There are several ways to insure a good strong spark besides going to a magneto, which is outside the beginner's class. The first thing to do is thoroughly check the ignition system, starting with the battery.

Follow through on this check list:

1. Check the battery for full charge.
2. Check battery connections for a tight fit, clean the terminals and the top of the battery. Loose or dirty connections offer resistance and lower the juice.
3. Check all wiring to the ignition switch and coil. Look for cracked insulation, oil-soaked wires, and loose connections.
4. Test the coil. If you have increased compression, you might need to go to a heavy-duty coil.
5. Check wiring to distributor, making sure that the ter-

minals fit securely into the coil terminal and the top terminal of the distributor.
6. Inspect the distributor cap for cracks, dirt, and poor connections.
7. Check the distributor carefully, including points, rotor, centrifugal and vacuum spark advances, etc. This is a standard tune-up procedure; detailed instructions are given in shop manuals and there are also complete books, as long as this one, devoted just to tune-up alone.
8. Check the spark-plug wire for good fit, clean terminals, and condition of the insulations.
9. Finally, check out the plugs.

In the normal course of operation the spark plugs take a terrific beating and are one of the greatest sources of lost power in an automobile engine. The high-tension electrical surge comes from the distributor down through the center electrode in the spark plug. It then jumps the gap to the grounded or outer electrode. To function properly these electrodes must be clean and unfouled by oil or carbon deposits. In addition, they must be the proper distance apart —properly gapped, a mechanic will say.

The Spark Gap

Setting the gap on a new plug is simple enough. You put a feeler gauge into the gap and bend the grounded electrode until the gap is correct.

The trouble is that the gap won't stay where it was bent. To find out why, we have but to consider what these two electrodes extending down below the base of the spark plug have to go through. In an engine idling at, say, 500 rpm, the electrodes will be hammered by full engine compression and then by the searing force of the burning gas mixture 125 times each minute. Then if you step up to 4,000 rpm, the plugs take this punishment one thousand times a minute.

When one considers what kind of a beating spark plugs take, the wonder is not that electrodes burn away and carbon forms, but that the plugs do as well as they do.

Hot and Cold Spark Plugs

The first thing of importance is to select the right plug. The manufacturer has generously listed the correct *heat range* of plug for you. Heat range means either hot plugs or cold plugs. For some reason, many beginners seem to think that this means plugs with a hotter or colder spark. It has nothing to do with the spark at all. The business end of a plug is heated first by the compression stroke and then by the burning gases in the power stroke, and finally by the blast of hot carbon rushing out during the exhaust stroke. A plug designed to pass this heat on to the head and water jacket more quickly is known as a *cold plug*. One that doesn't get rid of the heat as fast is called a *hot plug*. Depending upon the design, there are various degrees between the hottest and the coldest plug.

As we said before, the manufacturer will tell you what temperature plugs to use—in his stock engine. When you start tinkering and improving, you may have to change the heat range of your plugs.

For high-speed operations you want the coldest plug your mill will accept. However, these cold plugs will foul up fast when used under street conditions.

Too many factors must be figured in to give a hard-and-fast rule on plug selection for reworked engines. Therefore, the general advice experienced hot rodders pass along to beginners is to start with the recommended plug for the stock version of your mill. From this beginning you go step by step through the range of colder plugs until carbon fouls the electrodes. Then back off one grade.

If your plugs are too hot, the electrodes will be worn. The porcelain insulation in the center will be white instead of tanning out as is normal after a hundred miles or so of running.

However, if an inspection of the plugs show evidence of overheating, don't get colder plugs until you make a few checks. Incorrect timing, a clogged cooling system, and a too-lean carburetor mixture can also cause this trouble.

Another word of caution about heat and plugs. If the gasket ring is not put in right, it can cause a heat rise also.

Cams, Spark, and Exhaust ○ 101

Spark plugs should be carefully gapped with a feeler gauge, but you cannot follow the automaker's specifications if the mill has been modified. If a car's compression has been increased, it is usually necessary to decrease the gap to make up for the added resistance of the more tightly packed fuel.

Install the rings with the smooth side against the plug. Also there is an effect on the heat range of a plug if it is not tightened correctly. Plugs should be set in with a torque wrench according to the recommendations of the plug manufacturer.

Gapping the plugs, an essential part of any tune-up, should follow the builder's recommendations for an unworked engine only. When you up a car's compression, it is usually necessary to use a smaller gap between the electrodes to make up for the added resistance of the more tightly packed fuel.

More About Points

Let's go back for a minute to the ignition circuit. Previously we described the normal circuit where the primary circuit is broken by contact points. When the points open, the magnetic field in the primary circuit collapses in the coil, causing a high voltage in the secondary circuit of the coil.

This type of ignition system has its limitations because of the limited ability of the contact points in the distributor. The voltage output drops as engine speed decreases. Also the rapid opening and closing of the points at high speed limits the primary current flow which is necessary to building the magnetic field in the coil. The transistorized ignition system was developed to overcome these difficulties and to sustain voltage regardless of the engine speeds attained in today's high-compression engines.

Transistorized Circuits

A transistor acts like an electronic tube—the radio vacuum tube being the most familiar example. It is much smaller than the vacuum tube and does not need a vacuum to operate. It is used to control electron flows.

A diagram of a transistorized circuit looks very much like the regular ignition system with a transistor placed in the circuit between the coil and the points. However, there is a radical difference in operation. In the conventional system the primary circuit is broken when the points open. In the transistorized circuit, the transistor opens and closes the primary circuit.

There is still a need for the contact points. They trigger the transistor. This is done by a very light trigger current that flows up through the ground to the transistor. As long as the points are closed, this light current (from 0.5 to 1.0 ampere) triggers the transistor and permits the primary current to flow through the primary winding of the coil, inducing the necessary magnetic field. Then when the rubbing block in the distributor breaks the points, the transistor, no longer receiving the triggering current, breaks the primary circuit.

Then the magnetic field collapses as in the standard circuit. The freed electrons are collected by the secondary windings and the high-tension voltage necessary for a hot spark flows to the plugs.

The transistorized system requires a different coil from that used in the standard systems. It does not vary in principle, but only in the ratio of windings in the primary and secondary circuits.

8

ENGINE SWAPS

"Yeah, we'll admit that boring, stroking, porting, and all the rest of the tricks will throw an extra kick in the old mill, but how about taking a shortcut. What about an engine swap? Won't we get the same rewards with a fraction of the work?"

This question always crops up when you talk to a beginning group. What *about* engine swaps? Are they the answer to all our problems?

Well, they might be—*if* you know what you are going after and a bigger engine fits the bill. Unfortunately, like every other solution hot rodders come up with for their problems, this answer does not always work. Instead of solving problems, engine swaps often hit us squarely with a set of new puzzles to unravel.

Horsepower-to-Weight Ratio

Now the basic reason for increasing the cubes of a stock engine is to get *big engine displacement from a smaller engine*. Greater displacement means more horsepower without an appreciable increase in weight. No matter how much you argue, you can't get away from the fact that it takes more horses to pull a heavier vehicle than it does a lighter one. Throw off as much weight as you can, and let the horses expend their power going faster instead of pulling dead weight.

Now we are coming to something called *horsepower-to-*

weight ratio. This simply means how much horsepower are we getting for each pound of weight which that horsepower has to move over the street, dragstrip, or race course. Let's say we have a heap that weighs in at 3,400 pounds. The mill generates 300 horsepower. Our vehicle horsepower-to-weight ratio is 11.3 to 1. This is pretty close to normal for average street cars. Any kind of an engine swap that will increase this ratio may not be what we're looking for.

The horsepower-to-weight ratio is not our only consideration. The weight itself, without its effect on the ratio, may be a stumbling block. For example, the hemi-head Chrysler engines that came out in the early 1950's were top hot-rod favorites for a long time. The 392-cube version tipped the scales, without flywheel or clutch, at something around 775 pounds. The Chevvy II's four-cylinder engine weighed not over 350 pounds. You can readily see without an adding machine that this is more than twice the weight of the Chevvy II's 153-cube mill. It would appear that squeezing a brute like the hemi into the light Chevvy would give us the ultimate in power. After all, haven't we doubled our horsepower?

That may be true, but at the same time you have added 425 extra pounds to the front of that car. The suspension would never support it. You probably couldn't beef it up enough to handle that kind of weight. Even if you ripped it all out and rebuilt from scratch, there is the impossible job of trying to steer such a light car with a nose that heavy.

Cautions on Engine Swapping

Engine swappers are fond of saying you can put anything in anything—if you are determined enough. No doubt you can, but you are crazy to try it. There are certain popular swaps that can easily and profitably be made. These are simplified by standard conversion kits that join up the new engine and the power train in the old chassis. Most kits of this kind also contain the necessary altered motor mounts.

Here all you have to do is pull the engine, put in the replacement, and hook it up. That is, if the new engine fits the motor compartment. Even then you don't have any major problem because—if it is a popular swap—somebody has already solved the problems for you. It is just a matter of following instructions.

Engine-swapping originated with hot rodders in their Model A's, and since that time the Ford in all its forms has been the basic element in engine swaps. This is mainly so because of the ease with which the swap engine can be mated with the Ford transmission. Enthusiasts insist that you can stuff any kind of an engine in a Ford. This isn't exactly true, but at one time or another you'll see Fords with Buick, Cadillac, Chevrolet, Chrysler, DeSoto, Dodge, Lincoln, Mercury, Oldsmobile, Plymouth, Pontiac, and Studebaker mills grinding away under their hoods. And of course, swapping Ford for Ford is also popular if the owner wants to build up from a small V-8 to a huskier brute.

Engine-swapping is no bargain-basement way to get more horses. Prices vary with age, condition, and demand. So don't depend upon the following figures, offered here just to give you an idea. See your friendly used-engine dealer and start bargaining.

As an average, a Chevrolet 283 OHV can be bought secondhand for somewhere in the range between $100 and $250. A Ford V-8 OHV 332–428 ranges from $200 to $360. Buicks might range up to $450. The others fall into pretty much the same range. These prices should get you a motor in good condition. However, it probably will not be the condition you want. So figure this as only the base price from which you will build.

You'll also have to add on the adapter price, which will probably average from $50 to $75.

It is hard to say what extra work you will have to do. One swapper reported that he updated his '50 Merc ten years with a '60 Buick V-8. The only extra work involved drilling the Buick flywheel to accept the Ford clutch assembly.

Henry would certainly be surprised to see what has been done to his 1923 Model T. The original 4-cylinder mill has been replaced with a 324-cubic-inch Oldsmobile Rocket engine topped by dual quad carbs. Headers and gleaming chrome collectors replace the old exhaust. Even the radiator shell has been chromed. Such cars, while they are often driven on the street for fun, are primarily show vehicles. Specializing in show cars is a legitimate and interesting hot rod hobby.

Measurements Come First

The first step in engine swapping is neither buying the replacement mill nor removing the old one. Before doing anything else *measure* your engine compartment and insure

The Corvair engine is popular for off-the-rod rods and dune buggies because it is light and inexpensive, as engines go. This one provides the get-up-and-go for an open rail job.

that the engine you want will fit into it. The boys that tell us you can put anything into anything are absolutely right —but what they don't tell us is what kind of butchery is sometimes needed.

Occasionally you'll find a stubborn chap who intends to have a certain engine and will settle for nothing else. Generally these determined gents have spent a mint on customizing their bodies and intend to keep it, come what may. The march of progress has passed by their mills and all the other rodders are passing them too. If they won't settle for an easy swap—and quite a number won't—then the acetylene welder is their best friend. They're in for a lot of cutting and resettlement of supports, frame members, and accessories. Sometimes it also means relocation of the firewall. In the end you'll wind up paying more than what you end up with is worth.

If you get one of these boys who has gone through the agony of a difficult swap to stop lying and tell you the truth, most of them will say, "I'm glad I did it, but *never again!*"

Another thing that leaves them discouraged is that the swap often fails to produce the runaway power the swapper anticipated. What happened was that he knew somebody who was getting 110 mph from such a mill. He rushes out and crams the same engine in his old body, but can't even break a hundred. Why? Body design, the type of power train he has, gearing, and the like may be holding him back. Sometimes it is cheaper to buy a later-model car than it is to try and build up an older one.

Now back to our measuring. Suppose we have a heap with a small Ford V-8 260 and we are thinking of getting stylish with a Caddy big V-8, operating on the assumption that if a Ford is good, a Fordillac would be better. A comparison measurement will show that the small Ford mill is about 22 inches high, 28 inches long, and 21 inches wide. The length measurements include the fan pulley and the bellhouse. The Caddy big V-8 we were thinking about is 23 inches high, 28 inches long, and 28 inches wide.

The two engines are the same length. The extra inch in height will not bother us. But what about the extra seven inches in width? Can we cram the engine in anyway? What about steering-gear clearances? What about the battery? Will it have to be relocated? The position of the starter—which side it is located on—must also be considered. So must the oil filter. Also, there is the problem of clearance of the oil pan. Will it bump heads with the tie rods?

Then there is the exhaust to consider. Will the headers have to cut so sharply around obstructions that power-robbing back pressure is created?

Failure to consider all these potential troublemakers is the reason some swappers find themselves going in for more hacking and cutting than they bargained for. The result is that the expense mounts alarmingly.

The thing to do is to first decide on what you would *like* to do. Then check with your speed shop—in person or by mail if you live out of town. Find out if a conversion kit is available for the combination you want. If you have a Ford or Chevvy, almost any engine can be made to fit in and there is usually adapter kits available.

Beyond these two old reliables, except for the Mercury, kits start getting scarce, and are often only available for certain model years.

How to Remove and Replace Engines

Removing the engine for swapping is not difficult, but should be done with care and proper regard for safety. A chain hoist is an essential. You are lifting weights that range from 350 to nearly 800 pounds. Chain hoists can be obtained from rental tool places. Your main concern will be a place strong enough to hang it. If you are working in the family garage, never throw the hoist on an unsupported beam. Adding more timber support or a steel crossbeam is a must.

If you don't anticipate having much need for a hoist in the future, it might be well to rent an A-frame. It will be cheaper than reinforcing the roof beams. An A-frame is a tubular metal stand to support the hoist.

The A-frame has one distinct advantage. It is usually mounted on casters for easy movement. If you don't know how that helps, you've never pulled an engine with a stationary hoist and then tried to figure out how to get the mill across to the work bench. It sure helps to have a rolling A-frame.

The first thing to do is strip the mill as much as possible. Remove the hood. Drain the water from the radiator and the oil from the pan. Disconnect the water hoses and remove the radiator if necessary to get clearance when you hoist the engine out. If you are going to a much bigger engine, it may be necessary to put in a larger radiator anyway to keep the mill from overheating.

Engine Swaps ○ 111

Now take out the battery. You'll have to disconnect the coupling that connect with the dashboard gauges, the fuel line, and the air cleaner. Headers must be removed and so must the clutch and gearshift linkage.

Then before you remove the mounting bolts, make a last check to be sure that nothing sticks out that will impair

If you remove an engine for swapping, it might be worth renting an A-frame to support the chain hoist. Most hot rodders have difficulty finding a spot strong enough to safely support a powerplant that can weigh in at a quarter of a ton or more. Another advantage of the A-frame is that it has casters which permit easy movement.

clearance when you start lifting. It might be something like an oil filter you forgot.

A Chain Hoist Is a Must

On overhead-valve engines the usual procedure is to hitch your hoist onto the bolts holding the intake manifolds. This gives you pretty good weight balance.

When you start to lift, tighten the chain on the hoist slowly. Watch carefully to see that the chain links aren't kinked, and that your hoist is directly over the engine. If it isn't directly overhead, the angled pull could throw the rising engine against the side of the engine compartment.

If there is any danger of this, or if the engine droops so that the carbs linkage hits against the hoist chains, then you had best jerk off the carbs before you go on lifting. There is no real reason for putting off their removal until the engine is out of the chassis except that it is easier to work with the mill on the work bench.

Once the engine is removed, we begin working. If the exchange is a simple one, we'll only have to put on any necessary adapters to fit the motor mounts. If major surgery is indicated, this is the time to hack and saw and weld.

On some short engines it may be necessary to move the radiator back so it won't sit so far from the engine fan. On the other hand, if the engine is much longer than the one it replaces, you may have to move the firewall back to accommodate it.

As for connecting the flywheel to the clutch and transmission, the popular adapter kits come with instructions. Just follow them. Trying to pick your own way on models for which no kits are available is not for beginners. But if you must do it, then try to find a back issue of some hot-rod magazine that tells you how to go about the job.

Drive-Shaft Modifications

There are times when swapped transmissions or rear ends will require you to alter the drive shaft to make it fit. Sometimes a long engine will require us to shift everything back, and this also means shorting the drive shaft. The drive shaft—or propeller shaft—connects the transmission with the rear end. It conducts the torque developed by the crankshaft to the differential gear in the rear end.

At this point we run head-on into a basic auto design problem. The engine is rigidly bolted on its rubber mounts. On the other hand, the spring-loaded rear end bounces up and down as the car speeds over the road. This means that a rigid propeller shaft is out of the question. So universal joints are mounted at each end of the drive shaft on modern cars to allow the drive shaft to flex with the car's movement. Older cars sometimes had only one universal joint. The drive shaft itself may be a hollow tube connecting the two U-joints, or it may be a "torque tube drive" which means a solid shaft inside a hollow tube.

If you have to shorten the drive shaft, the hollow tube is the easiest to handle. The U-joint consists of two knuckles set at right angles to each other and connected together with a cross-shaped spider. There is a spline on the knuckle connecting with the transmission output shaft which permits the joint to slide back and forth (but not turn so that the torque is locked in) and take care of any lengthening or shortening as the car moves. The second knuckle is inserted in the hollow drive shaft and welded in place. This knuckle is removed, the shaft shortened, and the knuckle rewelded in place. In the torque-tube drive shaft, the solid shaft must also be shortened.

This is not an especially difficult job or a costly one. However, it calls for precision and an expert knowledge of welding. You just can't rent a welder and bluff your way through on something this important. You'll have to worry about realignment, getting a strong weld, and warping of the metal due to uneven heat. So it is best to take this kind of job to a pro and get it done right.

In some cases it may not be necessary to cut your shaft. By shopping around in wrecking yards you may find one that is the right length. The yard should have a copy of heaven's greatest gift to the hot rodder—an interchangeable-parts list.

This will help considerably in any kind of parts hunt. When you find the right length, it is probable that the knuckle or yoke won't connect up with the one on your transmission output shaft. So you cut through the weld on your new part —and *just* through the weld. Don't cut into the yoke. Then the yoke can be slipped out. Your old one is inserted and rewelded.

In shortening torque tubes like those used on the pre-1949 Fords, the outer hollow tube is shortened as noted above. The usual recommendation for the solid shaft is not to try and cut and weld it, but to cut it off at the end and have new splines cut for you by a machine shop.

If a drive shaft is not reworked carefully, you are going to have vibration, noise, and possible failure. The vibration may be caused by lack of balance. One side is heavier than the other, which causes the vibration when the shaft spins. Rebalancing is best done in a machine shop.

However, I know one mechanic who does it this way: he jacks up the rear wheels on *stands*. Then he puts the lightest clamp he can get around the shaft and inserts a washer under it on the lighter side of the drive shaft. Then he kicks the throttle up to about 50 mph. He then continues to adjust the position of the weight or the size of the washer until the vibration dampens. Later the washer can be spot-welded to the shaft for permanent balance.

I have never tried this myself, and feel it is no substitute for a professional balance job. However, if you feel like doing it, be specially careful to support the rear end on stands. Never depend upon jacks to hold your car up. Also, I don't feel easy about that washer unless it is securely bound to the shaft. It has the force of a bullet if it comes loose.

There is another safety matter to consider before we move on to the rear end. This is possible U-joint failure during high-speed competition. National Hot Rod Association rules require a safety loop—a steel band—under the drive shaft. If a U-joint goes out, this band will keep the front end of the rear part of the shaft from digging into the track and wrecking the car. It is not a bad idea to put the loop on your street rod.

National Hot Rod Association rules require a steel band safety loop under the front end of the rear part of the drive shaft. If a U-joint fails, this band will keep the shaft from dropping into the track and wrecking the car.

Rear-End Problems

Moving on back to the rear axle, we come to a very important part of any car, and one that has received a lot of attention from hot rodders. This is the "rear end" or differential.

The job of the rear end is to take the straight-line torque transmitted by the drive shaft and turn it at opposite right angles to run the rear wheels. This then brings up another design problem. With straight, even gearing both back wheels will turn at the same speed all the time. This is fine on the straightaway, but no good on turns. In a turn the outside wheel has to travel farther than the inside wheel. It can only keep up by turning faster.

This is where the differential comes in. It employs a unique set of spider gears that come into action only when the car is turning. At least that is the theory. When the inside turns slower on a curve, the spider gears are idling, which causes the opposite axle to turn faster. So far everything is fine. This is what we want it to do. But this same shift of power occurs when one wheel suddenly turns faster than the other. Let one wheel start to spin on a slippery surface and the other wheel stops. You lose all your traction. Car builders developed a type of locking differential to overcome this slipping through a type of pressure clutch. This works to prevent a car from stopping if one wheel slips, but is overcome on a turn so the outer wheel can still turn faster.

The power flow into a rear end comes through the drive shaft. A splined gear on the end of this shaft meshes with a pinion gear, which in turn meshes with a ring gear bolted to the axle.

The ratio between the pinion drive gear and the ring gear determines the amount of force that is applied to the wheels. A one-to-one ratio means that the wheels would turn at the same rpm as the drive shaft. This would be a very high gear indeed. But if we add more teeth to the ring gear, then the wheels will turn at fewer rpm than the drive shaft. The more teeth there are on the ring gear than on the pinion, the more leverage there is and the more power that can be applied to the wheels. This is why we start a car in low gear instead of high. There isn't enough power in high to get the car rolling.

Transmission gears can be changed either by shifting or by an automatic transmission, but rear-end gears are fixed at a predetermined ratio for the best general operation under the loads and conditions expected of the vehicle. This ratio varies from 3.4 to 1 to 5.0 to 1. Experimental ratios sometimes go beyond this.

As a general rule, the lower the gear (that is, the higher the ratio number), the quicker the vehicle gets under way. In drag racing this is bread and butter. So dragsters are geared for ratios of 5.0 and above.

Such low gear ratios are out of the question for street use. The rpm at cruising speed would have to be enormous.

Engine Swaps ○ 117

To understand this, put a stock car in low and listen to the bang of the engine at the top speed you can get in that gear. Then shift to second and notice the rpm drop at the same speed and so on into high. For street use—and maybe a little competition in the street class—3.90 to 1 is about it.

Quick-Change Rear End

To overcome the trouble of being locked in with a set rear-end ratio, the quick-change rear end was developed. This involves changing the center section. The quick-change set (made by Halibrand Engineering, Torrance, California) can be swapped in five minutes.

To change the ratio under this system, drain the oil from the quick-change housing, take off the back plate, and remove

The Halibrand quick-change kit on this rear axle permits rapid changing of rear-end gear ratios. Complete change can be done in five minutes.

the old gears from their splines. Then slide the new gears on, button it up, and pour the lubricant back in. If you are of a mind and think you need it, you can get gear sets that will go from 1 to 1 to 7 to 1.

It should be kept in mind that quick-changes are for competition machines. You don't need them for the street. For straight street driving, the overdrive is your best bet. Here you bypass the regular transmission gearing for a more direct drive. This further reduces your engine speed while maintaining the same car speed. Call it a "high high" gear, if you wish.

The overdrive has been around for a long time, but has always been a part of the transmission, except for some truck two-speed rear ends used on heavy-duty haulers. Big trucks need very low gearing to get their heavy loads moving from a dead stop, but need higher gearing to keep from having to crawl to their destination.

Lately there have been signs that manufacturers are moving in for rear-end overdrives. One is on the market and two others have been announced as in the development stages. Just what they will lead to is not clear at this time, but rear-end overdrives may well be the next hot item in hot rodding.

9

SUSPENSION

The idea of an automobile suspension system is to smooth out the ride. This makes things easier on the rider and the car itself, preventing both from being shaken to pieces by the jolts and bumps.

In this respect Detroit has done a pretty good job of compromising between comfort and the best kind of handling. For souped-up speeds the normal suspension is too soft. It has to be toughened up, but this will always be at the expense of comfort. You can't have both, so don't waste time worrying about it.

For the sake of simplifying things, we'll call the suspension system the springs and shock absorbers, plus the tires. Actually the tires are a car's first line of defense against jolts, and the entire idea of pneumatic tires—those holding air—is to make things easier on the bumpy road.

Tires—Good and Bad

Tires, of course, have another and more important role than absorbing bumps. This is *traction*. And traction is what moves the car. All that fancy souping from cubes to quick-change in the tail goes for nothing if the tires don't grip the road.

Here again the final answer just isn't there. Tires must be chosen for the job they are going to do, and there is no one tire that will fit them all. The present trend in all types of tires is toward a wider tread. Wide-tread street tires in turn demand a wider space between the tread design. This is not to grip the road better, as many seem to think. It is so the wider tread can squeeze out water faster as it runs on wet streets and thus improve poor-weather running.

One of the biggest mistakes a beginner can make is to rush out and put racing tires on his new wagon. This happens all too often for overgrown tires, and magnesium wheels seem to raise any heap into the upper-bracket performance class. Unfortunately it takes more than looks. Racing tires are not made for streets. Slicks are out because states insist on tread for safety's sake. Some even regulate the legal depth of this tread, so this rules out "cheater slicks" which have a very light tread in their soft rubber. These tires are for stock-class dragsters. For the street rod, just stick with an ordinary tire—but get the best you can afford.

Cheap tires are no bargain. Also avert your eyes and hurry past the local service station advertising recaps, unless they are racing recaps, which are something else. All it takes is one blowout and a roll in the ditch to cost more than you'll save on cheap tires in a long, long time.

Racing tires are made with much less rubber than street tires and usually carry much higher pressure. If you try to use them on the street, they'll wear out faster and give you a spine jarring ride as a bonus.

Wheels

The wheels themselves are something to consider also. The so-called "mag wheels" usually aren't. Mag (for "magnesium") originally meant that they were made of magnesium alloy for lightness. In racing, the more weight you can toss out the less there is to pull, and easing up on unsprung weight is a way to improve handling as well.

But mag wheels are expensive. So many of the so-called mags are either aluminum or prettied-up steel. Very little weight saving comes through with them. For most practical purposes they are just for show. This is okay, too, if you like it that way.

Springs—Front and Rear

The springs of a car support its weight and absorb a lot of the bounce to keep the frame from shaking to pieces.

Racing slicks—soft rubber without tread—are strictly for the tracks. They are illegal on the streets. This one is on Don Prudhomme's Wynn's Winder, a slingshot dragster. The slingshot is so called because the driver sits out behind as if he were merely an afterthought of the designer. The blown Plymouth fuel injection engine can be seen just over the slick.

Most cars today use coil springs in the front and leaf springs in the back. Coil springs permit a front-end construction that allows each of the front wheels to move up and down independently of the other. Although you don't hear the term much anymore, this was originally called "knee action."

Up until about 1934 all cars had straight axles in front. The wheel pivoted on a solid shaft called a *kingpin*. The knuckle holding this was firmly attached to the straight axle. Thus if one wheel ran over an obstruction in the road, the entire car tilted. Knee action permits one wheel to raise while the frame remains level.

Springs are supposed to absorb road shock, but unfortunately once they start to bounce they don't want to stop. So shock absorbers—*shocks,* in auto language—are used to control the spring action. The shock is a telescoping tube partially filled with fluid. Hydraulic action of the fluid working through a restricted opening inside the tube slows down the action. This dampens the bouncing of the spring. You can check the proper action of a shock by bouncing a front fender. If it stops quickly, the shocks are in good order. If the bouncing continues, it's time for new shocks.

For hot rodding, you'll need stiffer suspension and heavy duty shocks to increase stability. Stock equipment is designed for a soft ride. You'll have to sacrifice some of this for stability.

The only way to get stiffer action from your shock has been to replace them in the past. Lately adjustable shock absorbers have started to appear on the market. They are all pretty expensive and haven't been around long enough to have made much impression on the hot-rodding fraternity.

Some hot rodders put extra leaves in their rear springs to help hold the road at high speeds. These are usually accompanied by an adjustable shackle. This permits different spring positions which can give some change in weight distribution.

Another springing help is the torsion bar. This is a rod of spring steel mounted on each side of the front end. One end of the torsion bar is mounted at the lower control arm and the other is securely attached to the frame. The front end then is able to move with the wheel. Since the back end is fixed to the frame, the bar twists with the up-and-down movement of the wheel. The spring action comes because the spring steel bar resists the twisting and returns to its original position. This spring action absorbs wheel shocks.

Brakes

While we are talking about wheels might be as good a time as any to get in a word or two about brakes. In their enthusiasm for moving in a hurry, too many beginners give **no** thought to the fact that they have to stop sometime—and

This extension spring shackle provides space to adjust the spring to take care of different weight shifts during acceleration. Weight shifts strongly to the rear during fast takeoffs.

often with unexpected suddenness. The higher the speed of a car, the more efficient the braking system must be. Unfortunately there is no brake good enough to do what it needs to do.

The oldest brake we know of was on the wagons, coaches, and buggies. It was nothing more than a lever mounted so that the driver could operate it by hand or foot. Operating this caused a bar or arm to press a rubbing block against the tire. The friction slowed down the vehicle. Basically that is exactly what we use on cars today. There are two major refinements over the brake of the days when horsepower really meant *horse* power. One is that we no longer press the rubbing block against the tire. It is pressed against the inside of a brake drum and the rubbing block is now called the *brake shoe*.

The other big change is that we now use a hydraulic system instead of brute force to push the brake up against the moving wheel.

When you press the pedal of a hydraulic brake the foot pedal actuates a piston in the master hydraulic cylinder. This piston forces hydraulic fluid through the brake lines to smaller cylinders at each wheel. The fluid pressure in the wheel cylinders push against links which force the brake shoes against the brake drums. The friction slows the car in exactly the same manner as the wooden block stopped the covered wagon—but a lot more efficiently, of course.

A scientist named Pascal stated the scientific law that permits hydraulic brakes to work. According to Pascal's law a fluid in an enclosed system will transmit pressure *equally* in all directions and will exert an equal force on any equal surface. This means that when you step on an hydraulic brake, you'll get equal force at all four wheels.

Brake Troubles

The old mechanical brakes used before hydraulics became standard on automobiles could not do this. It was almost impossible to keep all wheels adjusted equally.

While hydraulic brakes have the advantage of greater reliability, greater stopping power, and even pressure on all wheels, they are not yet the answer to the stopping problem. The trouble is *friction heat*. If you remember your high school physics, you can't destroy energy. You only change it from one form to another. In stopping you change kinetic energy—moving energy—to heat energy. If this heat builds up too much in the brakes, it causes the drums to expand unevenly. Heat causes metal to expand, you know. At the same time you are putting high pressure on the expanding drum. This eventually knocks the drum out of round. Also heat plus friction wear will cause the brake linings to become smooth and lose their bite on the drums. When these things happen, we get what is known as *fade*. You don't always have to run brakes for years for this to happen. Try a few panic stops and you'll start getting some fade.

The solution to fade—which is a very serious problem with high-performance cars—is to get rid of the heat. Keep the brake cool. In the old days when cars sat up as if on stilts and we had spoke wheels, a large volume of air could circulate around the brake drum. Today we have lowered the silhouette, fancied up the wheels until very little air can circulate through them, and increased braking surface to produce even more heat.

Keep Them Cool

Radiation is the only way these brakes have of getting rid of heat. They need air and plenty of it blowing past the heated drum to carry this heat away.

This means that you should stay away from wheel covers that cut out air and stick with the most open wheel you can get. Gimmicks for cooling brakes pop up every now and then. Almost everyone, faced with the problem for the first time, starts thinking about air cooling the drums by using fins like those on a motorcycle engine. If you have such thoughts, don't bother to rush to the patent office. It's been thought of before. The trouble is that modern cars are designed not for efficiency but for appearance. There is no room to put air-cooled fins on these brakes. Nor will you solve the problem by going to bigger drums because there isn't room for them either.

With certain cars it is possible to increase the brake size somewhat. Several manufacturers (Ford and Chevrolet are examples) make special police cars which are built for heavy-duty work. They have special brakes that resist fading. They can be swapped on similar make cars with little difficulty.

Disc Brakes

The coming thing, however, in brakes is the caliper disc brake. Here the brake drum is a metal disc. Sitting over the top of the disc is a caliper which may be likened to a metal hood. Its sole purpose is to hold hydraulic pistons and brake-

GM

Souped-up cars need brakes that resist fading. This disc brake can do considerably better than the old drum brake.

lining pads. When pressure is applied on the brake pedal, fluid through the brake lines force the pistons forward and the pads are pressed against *both* sides of the brake disc. Where drum brakes press from the inside out against the brake drums, the disc brake presses from the outside in. It is like clamping the brake disc in a vise.

Disc brakes have the advantage of resisting fading more than drum brakes. They run cooler naturally, but where a drum brake fades at 1200 degrees Fahrenheit, the disc brake is still gripping at 1500 degrees F. Since they work better at higher temperatures, the early discs had a tendency to grab and squeak at low-temperature driving. This has about been eliminated in later-model brakes.

But there is a snake in every Eden. Several years of trials in sports cars have shown that the rigid-mounted caliper disc brakes have their faults too. One fault that appeared was rotor wobble. Warping of the disc rotor knocked back the hydraulic piston, causing it to pulsate.

Another trouble, of special interest to hot rodders, is that hard cornering sometimes caused twisting in the front end that pushed the discs against their pistons.

Detroit's answer to this has been a "floating" caliper which has a flexible joint between the caliper and its mount. These were introduced in 1969 and are still too new to have revealed any inherent flaws.

Disc brakes, however, have been around long enough to start appearing on older-model cars within the financial reach of a beginner. They should be given a thorough overhaul because they are surely worn. Overhaul is not difficult. Generally all you can do is replace the worn rotor and put on new brake-lining pads. Overhauling the caliper itself is a job for the brake shop.

10

CUSTOMIZING

Some years ago an automobile manufacturer had a TV commercial in which the announcer said that the company had asked one of Italy's greatest custom designers what they could do to improve their design. That caught our attention, because if ever a car needed a new design this was it.

The TV showed a thoughtful man followed by three anxious car executives walking around the company's pride and joy. After the inspection, the great designer said that he would just make the rear window larger.

"That's all?" the executives asked.

"That's all," the great designer replied.

And so, the announcer said that was all the company did. In fact, except for changing the bumper design, that is all the company has done since.

But if they *really* wanted to make a change, they should have called in a hot rodder. This dissatisfied-with-everything-stock breed can not only find more things to change than the rear window on a VW Bug, but can also find plenty to change on everything from a Cadillac to a Zilchmobile—if there is such a car.

Chopping—Channeling—Lowering

It all comes under the heading of "customizing" and means raising the appearance of a car out of the ordinary. Customizing, like the hemline on ladies' fashions, has its trends. Once a rodder just wasn't with it unless he was chopping,

128

channeling, and lowering. Today a lot of people don't even know what you're talking about if you use these once potent words. *Chopping* means cutting down the top so that the windows become little better than peepholes. *Channeling* is dropping the body down over the frame, while *lowering* uses U-bolts and lowering blocks to drop the back end for stylish rake.

These devices were all employed for the same reason—to make the tall models of the day look low and graceful. However, cars today are so low anyway that if you drop them any further you might just well throw away the wheels and install sleds or runners. On many cars with long overhang in the rear the tail almost drags on every dip. Lowering such a body is out of the question. Even when lowering had a place in hot-rod customizing, too many carried it to the extreme. Some hugged the road so closely that they were undrivable off a flat road.

The first step in customizing is to decide what you want to do with the car after it is dressed up. It all depends upon whether you'll drive the heap to work, hit the drag strips or stock-car tracks, or go after custom-car show trophies.

For street jobs you have to keep within legal limits, which means no straight exhausts, slicks, or undrivable cams. On the drag strips you'll have to conform with class limitations. The kind of body you slap on your chassis will determine in many cases where you fall. As far as decorating goes, if you haven't a bright paint job and enough decals to turn your heap into a rolling billboard, you are in danger of being regarded as a freak, a square, and a nonconforming screwball.

Show-Car Customizing

The show-car route is something else. These cars are admittedly beautiful things. The work and money that go into them is staggering. Even though most carry signs insisting they are driven regularly, these cars are luxuries that can break a beginner's back and bankroll fast. And I do mean break his bankroll. Recently at a Los Angeles custom

130   ○   **Hot Rodding for Beginners**

car show I saw a Model A that sold new for $400 with a $4,000 price tag on it. Considering the time and money that must go into this kind of customizing, it is probably well worth the price. However, it is not a good idea to spend this much on a car if just selling it for a profit is your aim. Buyers of these kinds of cars are not standing on every corner. Build them for advertising, for prestige of winning cups and trophies, or just because you like this sort of thing. Forget all other reasons.

If you have in mind a heap to haul you around town and turn some heads as you go by, then the sky is the limit, the sky being your pocketbook and your imagination. Actually, customizing technically would include anything you do that

"The Deuce"—a 1932 Ford—has been a hot rodder's favorite since the sport began on the streets and dry lakes of Southern California. This one has been "chopped" three inches. That is, the top has been cut off and lowered three inches. Chopping was a popular customizing trick on older cars, but later model cars are low enough as it is. The treadless racing slicks on the rear wheels show that this Deuce has been hopped-up for drag racing.

Extreme lowering of the car's body, once very popular with rodders, is now out of fashion. Low runners like this Caddy are difficult to drive over dips and sharp inclines because the tail drags.

gets away from stock, be it dabbing on some far-out paint or putting in a new cam. However, in this chapter we will narrow customizing down to improving—or at least changing —the appearance of the car.

You'll Need a Plan and a Model

The first thing to do is to make a careful plan, otherwise you may wind up with something that looks like an accident on its way to happen. Customizers usually suggest that a beginner make pencil sketches to firm up his design. This isn't much help to someone who can't draw. You might try making some grease-pencil marks over a photograph. Such marks will wipe off the glossy surface and you can keep hitting until trial-and-error produces something that strikes your eye.

Another recommendation is to use plastic model cars, then build up your ideas with modeling clay. This is easier than trying to sketch your ideas, and gives a better idea of what those airscoops you are thinking of will look on your heap's hood.

Here's another idea that works if you are thinking of swapping parts. It steals a trick from our artist friends, bu doesn't require any drawing ability. Occasionally you wi see an artist close one eye and hold a brush handle betwe his face and the subject. What he is doing is measuring the subject. We see depth—the three-dimensional effect—because we have two eyes. Close one eye and you lose depth. Hold your finger toward an object—say the fender of a car. With two eyes there is a lot of space between them. But if you close one eye, it will look as if your finger is actually touching the car even though it is at a distance. We'll use the same idea to test out ideas for our customizing.

Suppose we'd like to know how our car would look with a different type of grill. Find what you like in a car magazine, cut it out, hold it between your eyes and the front of your car, close one eye and assess the results.

Chances are you won't like it. You can't just stick anything on to everything. It has to harmonize, and fit in with the rest of the car. Actual installation is no real problem. You can cut down, alter, saw, and weld, so you can do just about anything you want—from putting a Cadillac grill on a VW to building a VW-type nose on a Ford. It is just a case of having sufficient determination—stubborness, if you will. But a silk top hat does not go well with a pair of blue jeans, nor does a dinner jacket harmonize with pajama bottoms.

Know What You Want and Why

This is why it is important to know what you want before you start. You can't experiment and keep changing your mind. It costs too much to make changes if you don't like the results. Anything you add to the car should look as if it was intended for that vehicle and belonged on it.

There is absolutely no point in change for change's sake. Stick with your heap's best points and change only what needs to be changed.

By all means look around and see what others are doing with models like yours. Don't feel you must be a complete rebel. It does not pay to go too far off the deep end. Styles in customizing change. As we mentioned earlier, chopping and lowering are now out of fashion. Another change is the attitude toward chrome. For a long time a hot rodder couldn't

Extreme lowering of the car's body, once very popular with rodders, is now out of fashion. Low runners like this Caddy are difficult to drive over dips and sharp inclines because the tail drags.

gets away from stock, be it dabbing on some far-out paint or putting in a new cam. However, in this chapter we will narrow customizing down to improving—or at least changing —the appearance of the car.

You'll Need a Plan and a Model

The first thing to do is to make a careful plan, otherwise you may wind up with something that looks like an accident on its way to happen. Customizers usually suggest that a beginner make pencil sketches to firm up his design. This isn't much help to someone who can't draw. You might try making some grease-pencil marks over a photograph. Such marks will wipe off the glossy surface and you can keep hitting until trial-and-error produces something that strikes your eye.

Another recommendation is to use plastic model cars, then build up your ideas with modeling clay. This is easier than trying to sketch your ideas, and gives a better idea of what those airscoops you are thinking of will look on your heap's hood.

Here's another idea that works if you are thinking of swapping parts. It steals a trick from our artist friends, but doesn't require any drawing ability. Occasionally you will see an artist close one eye and hold a brush handle between

This '37 Ford has been shaved and lightened for drag racing.

get the shiny stuff off his car body quick enough. But at the same time he piled all he could get on his engine.

Somehow the idea got around that dechroming made for smoother lines. Sometimes it did, but at other times the severe dechroming made the old boat look even more bulky. Trim is not stuck on a car blindly. Designers put it on to lead the eye. Often when it is removed the result is a big slab of metal that has lost a lot of its graceful look.

It is true, of course, that the glittering trim is often overdone. Some of it can certainly go on any model. If you dechrome because your trim is badly rusted and you don't want to go to the expense of replacing it, you can go the striping route if the dechroming leaves the car looking slab-sided. Plastic striping tape has taken the place of the old paint striping that took an expert to do right.

Customizing does not have to be overdone. Often just a change in the grill, mag-type wheels and a new paint job are all that you need to turn an old clunk into something that looks ten years younger.

Body Work of Various Kinds

Getting rid of radiator ornaments, makers' emblems, and trim takes a little more work then just jerking the stuff off and puttying up the holes. You just can't fill the holes with body putty and drive off. Putty has an annoying habit of popping out on you.

The best way to get it to stay put is to use the welding torch. The weld is then filed flush and sanded to a smooth finish. Throw on some paint and you're done.

If body solder is used, there is a definite technique to use. Maybe it would be well to tap a light dimple over the hole to be filled. Then when this is filled level with the metal and sanded it will leave a lip overhanging the actual hole. If the same lip is left on the inside, then you have something to keep the fill from moving out or in during the jolting of normal driving.

Body solder is giving way to epoxy plastics and new compounds, but the basic technique is the same. Clean the area to be soldered right down to the bare metal. If a hole is to be filled, be sure the inside of the hole is cleaned as well. Solder is not just spread on. It must be worked under low heat from a torch and smoothed on with a paddle after first tinning the area to be soldered. The best way to tin is to use a tinning compound which not only contains tin but also has a chemical cleaner. The tinning insures that the body solder sticks. The solder has to be kept plastic both during application and later when it is smoothed with the paddle. If it cools and you have to reheat it, the metal will have a granulated texture.

Rust, Dents, Fillers

Generally in working old cars one has to do quite a bit of body work. Rust and dents have to be taken out. Don't try to make body solder or plastic filler take the place of the hammer. The thicker these materials are applied, the more chance of them breaking, chipping, or falling out entirely.

This 1934 Ford is a beautiful job of hot rodding/restoring. Note the chopped top and the mirrored chrome firewall. However, the 1910 Overland, partly visible in the background, draws more attention at an auto show.

Leading (pronounced "ledding")—body solder—is preferable to plastics, although plastics can be applied easier and quicker.

Hammering dents from sheet metal is done with a dolly and a bumping hammer. Kits are available at any auto supply store. They are very reasonable. The dolly is held against the low part of the dent and the hammer bumps against the raised part.

One of the things that frustrates a beginner in body work is that he can never seem to bump the metal completely flat. The trouble is that when metal is struck a violent blow as when it is hit by another car, the metal is stretched. Some parts of the dent have thinned out while the top has thickened. The only way to get the final bump out is to shrink the metal.

This is done by heating the spot to a cherry red with the welding flame. It must be done carefully or the torch will burn through the metal. Then the cherry-red metal is struck two quick blows with a hammer. After that, back the spot with a dolly and hammer it flat.

Handling the torch may be beyond the ability of a beginner. If so, one should still learn to do his own bumping. Even if you have to take the job to a body shop for the final touches, the cost will be greatly reduced if you do most of the work yourself.

The Paint Job

Once the body work is completed, chrome removed, and any changes accomplished, the next step is painting. This is the moment of truth for the car customizer. No matter how great the rest of the work is, an amateurish paint job can degrade it all. Many customizers won't even tackle the painting themselves after their first unhappy experience. However, one never learns unless one plunges in and makes mistakes. Paint and lacquer are applied with spray gun. These can be rented. It is a good idea to ask a lot of questions when you rent it. You can pick up a lot of tips that will save you grief later.

Painting troubles can usually be isolated into three major divisions: improper handling of the spray, lack of proper preparation of the painting surface, and cleanliness.

Cleanliness means not only doing your work in a dust-free place, but keeping your equipment clean also. A bit of dried paint in the spray ports and nozzles can cause faulty air flow that will give poor patterns. Dirt can also cause uneven spraying. Another thing to watch for is cleanliness of the car itself. This seems self-evident. Every painter washes the car before spraying, but he doesn't always pay attention to one of the major sources of a poor paint job.

Water and dirt collect around moldings and trims and in

These two photographs of a '49–'50 Chevrolet give an indication of what a small amount of customizing can do to modernize an old car. Note that the sun visor has been removed, and the hood has been "shaved" by removing the chrome center strip, hood ornament and the maker's emblem. The holes were welded and the car repainted from its original gray to a canary yellow. Half the grill was retained after "teeth" were inserted for a different look. The bumper, which was badly bent after the first photograph was taken, was replaced with one from a later model Chevy. New wheels and whitewalls completed the simple custom job.

joints around the doors, windows, and hoods. Even though you have done a thorough wash job, it is still there. The blast from the spray gun often knocks it loose. Then you have a speckled job that nothing except removing the paint and redoing will cure. The solution is to use an air hose with a pressure nozzle to blow out all joints.

An unfortunate fact of the customizer's life is that paint will not cover imperfections. It molds right around them. There is no substitute for sanding. It is not necessary to sand down to the bare metal all over the car. Paint can be applied over paint—if the stock paint is sound.

The existing paint job should be checked with extra care. Look for rust blisters and sand them carefully to the base

Cleanliness is a must if you want to do a good paint job. Even though you have thoroughly washed the car, be sure to use a pressure-nozzle air hose to blast out all water and dirt that will still collect around moldings and trims and in joints around doors, windows, and hoods.

metal. All breaks in the paint must be feather-edged. This means smoothing down the break so there is no ridge left. If the paint is checked—that is, covered with hairline breaks—you'll have to get out the paint remover and get it all off. These hairlines mean that there is rust underneath.

Paint remover is generally flammable. It should be used in a place with plenty of ventilation. The remover is brushed on one panel at a time. When the paint softens, scrape it off with a paint scraper. Baked enamel may take two coats. Clean up after the scraping with a wire brush and steel wool. The bare metal is then cleaned with a solvent to insure that no grease or wax is on the metal after you completely sand the bare metal with fine sandpaper. Do not touch the metal after it has been cleaned. Oil from fingerprints will keep the paint from sticking and it will peel later.

Areas that will not receive paint are carefully masked. Then a primer-surfacer is sprayed on in several coats, allowing each coat to become dull-dry before applying the next. This prevents cracking. The primer-surfacer is wet-sanded with No. 320 paper after it has dried. The sanding dust is cleaned off and the car is at last ready for final painting. Incidentally, wear a nose mask for safety while using the spray.

Spray Painting Know-How

The secret of spray painting is to paint in sweeps with the gun at right angles to the metal and about eight inches above it. Each stroke overlaps the adjoining one by half its length. Work with a very light coat. The first one will barely cover the metal. When this coat is tacky, come back with a second and heavier coat. Follow this with still a third coat. Some pros insist on six coats. Anything over that is useless, since you have to keep color sanding.

Sand the car lightly with No. 400 sandpaper before applying the final coat. The final coat is similarly sanded to remove any nibs. Then the job is finished off with hand rubbing with medium rubbing compound. This brings out the lustre. Finally you top it all off by a dry buff with an electric buffer.

With practice one can become proficient with the spray painter, but interior finishing is something else. Despite many articles on how-to-do-it upholstery, I have yet to find a beginner who could do a really professional job. Cutting, sewing, shaping, and fitting is a monumental job. In Southern California a popular solution is to skip over to Tijuana, Mexico, and get the job done there. Even at below-the-border prices, the tag may make you blanch, but it is not as staggering as a Los Angeles job.

Interior Remodeling

This doesn't mean you have to pass up the interior completely. The dash is a fertile field for experimentation. I know one enthusiast who ripped out his instruments and put in a dash that looks as though it could navigate his heap to the moon and back.

Another threw out his steering-column shift and put it on the floor. He then built a console around it which was set between two bucket seats he picked up for a song at the wrecking yard. The results look like a top custom job and took very little work.

Getting rid of the column shift is a popular conversion on cars that don't have automatic transmissions. For hot rodding the floor shift is smoother and quicker. When you're dragging, every split second counts toward the money. Kits are available for these conversions. Most follow the familiar H pattern shift, but at least one kit was made with a single-plane shift that fitted nicely into a console. Easy-to-follow directions come with each kit, making this one of the simplest bolt-on jobs there is.

Fiber-Glass Body Building

The greatest single blessing ever to fall like manna from heaven into the grateful arms of automobile customizers is that wonderful material known as *glass fiber* (or sometimes reversed to *fiber glass*). Here at last is a material that can be shaped just about any way you want it. Where previously bodies had to be stamped out of metal, now you can do it yourself with plastics.

The idea is not new. As far back as 34 years ago Henry Ford Senior, keen on the notion of making things from soy

FORD MOTOR CO.

Henry Ford was hep to plastics a long time ago, as shown here swinging a sledge against a plastic panel to prove its durability. But this material was not practical for auto bodies until a suitable reinforcing agent was devised. Fibers of glass turned out to be the long-sought answer, and the result was that wonderful material known as fiber glass. For the hot rodder, this opened the door to spectacular do-it-yourself customizing or the building of entire bodies from scratch.

beans, used a plastic panel on a car of his and was photographed for the newsreels swinging a sledge against it. He proved its durability, but plastics had to wait until a practical method of reinforcing them could be devised. This turned out to be fibers of glass woven into mats, or formed into unwoven mats held together with a binder.

Combined with polyester resins, fiber glass proved to be the long-awaited answer to spectacular custom body building. Although Henry Ford started the ball rolling in Detroit in 1936, the automobile industry made only half-hearted attempts to develop plastic panels. The boat-building industry picked up the ball and scored a touchdown with it.

Then Chevrolet became the first to go into quantity production when it introduced the first true American sports car, the Corvette.

Glass-fiber body building is relatively simple. The major difficulty and the most time-consuming part of it is the necessity to build a mold over which to form the plastic sheets. But before going into the basics of mold making, let's talk first about the material used in glass-fiber body building.

First there is the glass fiber itself. It comes either as woven fabric or as unwoven mats. The mats are bound together with a weak binder so it can be handled. This material serves as the reinforcing material for the plastic.

The plastic is a polyester resin. It comes as a liquid which pours about like syrup. When mixed with a catalyst this liquid will polymerize or turn into a hard solid. This is called *curing.*

If heat is necessary for curing, an activator is mixed with the catalyst. It creates a chemical reaction with the catalyst. This forms sufficient heat to cause the catalyst to do its work in hardening the resin.

There have been various experiments with other types of materials for reinforcements. Nylon is one. Cotton has also been used. However, none have the strength-to-weight ratio of fiber glass. In other words, with other reinforcements you have to increase weight to get the same strength.

Body Building the Easy Way

Now we are ready to talk about the actual mechanics of building up the glass-fiber body. Before going any further, let's say a word about how easy it is. Is it really as simple as some writers make out? Can you really do it in your own

Customizing ○ 143

garage? Well, recently I had occasion to interview a man in the course of my newspaper work. He had just finished a two-year project building an automobile from scratch. It began as a family project with the sole idea of giving his teen-age son something to do that would keep him off the street. Neither he nor his son had any experience in this sort of thing.

The job turned out to be a neighborhood project instead of a family one. Every boy past crawling age came around to lend a hand.

"We built the body of fiber glass," the father said. "No, we did not have any experience. In fact, none of us had even seen anyone working with plastics. I went to a dealer who handles supplies. He gave me some literature and we just followed directions."

The result is stunning. The finished maroon sports body, constructed on a Volkswagen suspension with a Porsche mill, looks far better in person than it does in the accompanying photograph. It is a remarkable example of what can be accomplished with fiber glass even by the inexperienced.

A picture doesn't do justice to this truly beautiful car that was built as a family project. It started as a Volkswagen suspension; then a Porche engine was added. The body is homemade fiber glass. Parts of 14 makes of cars went into its final construction. It took two years to build.

144 ○ Hot Rodding for Beginners

There is not room here for a step-by-step description of the fiber-glass body-building process. However, we will sketch over it quickly to give you some idea of what you have to do if you want to go this route with your customizing.

Life-Size Plaster Mold

Again the first step is to decide what you want. Once you have your design in mind, you must construct a life-size plaster model. This model must be carefully constructed, for it will serve as the mold for our fiber-glass operations. The method we are describing is known as the *male-mold method*. This means that the body will be constructed by laying up sheets of fiber glass and resin on the outside of the mold.

First the mold is covered with a "parting agent" which prevents the fiber-glass body from sticking to the mold. This parting agent, after it dries, is then waxed for additional protection. The next step is to spray or brush on a coat of resin over the mold. After it cures, an additional coat is brushed on. While this is still tacky a sheet of fiber glass is pressed on and then saturated with resin. The resin—mixed with the catalyst, naturally—is poured on and then spread with a spreader as evenly as possible.

You then continue building up successive layers. Five layers are usually sufficient. After the body is pulled from the mold, it is possible to build up and strengthen any desired spot by laying up additional layers of fiber glass and resin on the inside.

The entire body, of course, is not built up at the same time. You work by sections and panels. Due regard must be made for opening doors, hoods, grill openings, etc. You can figure on around 15 gallons of resin and not over 40 yards of fiber-glass cloth for the average body.

Grinding the Shell

After the fiber-glass shell is removed from the mold, it is sanded smooth. Edges may have to be trimmed. It is best to use a power sander, but don't fail to wear a respirator when sanding or grinding fiber glass. The dust is extremely abrasive and you may find you are grinding your own respiratory system. Don't take any chances with this stuff. It's potent. Another safety tip: follow directions exactly when mixing the resin, catalyst, and promoter. Remember the purpose of the promoter is to generate internal heat through reaction with the catalyst. Improper mixing can start it heating at the wrong time, with explosive results. There is no danger if handled right—and handling right means *following directions.*

In grinding the shell to obtain a smooth surface, you may get down to the glass cloth in places. Remember, when you saturate the cloth in laying up the body, you cannot soak the resin into the glass fibers themselves. The binder penetrates around the tiny fibers. So grinding may cut through the covering resin in places. Don't worry about it. When you get done smoothing, re-cover the shell with a coat of activated resin. When this cures, add another coat. This is sanded smooth with fine sandpaper. Unexpected imperfections can be filled with plastic body putty.

Now you sand, prime, and paint as you would a metal body.

Body Parts Molding

It is not necessary, or even desirable, to begin work on a full body. Many get experience working on single panels or subassemblies. A new hood, built around a fancy grill, is a good way to get your feet wet. Fiber glass, being lighter, is a good way to reduce weight for dragging.

Just what to do to customize your heap is strictly up to you. As a beginning we might suggest something like this:

- A new hood and front fenders.
- Install bucket seats.
- Change from column to floor shift. If a straight-shift kit is available for your model, build in a console.
- Revamp the dashboard, adding a tachometer.
- Dechrome if necessary. Add striping to keep away from a slab appearance.
- Go to mag wheels and wider-tread tires. If your fender

146 ○ *Hot Rodding for Beginners*

wells are too small, it is not a big job to radius them out bigger.
- Repaint.
- On the interior, install new seat covers, repaint the metal, add a new floor mat, replace worn wind lacing. If the interior has a molded liner, you can repaint that with a matte paint.

It is better for a beginner to follow tried-and-true paths where the pioneering has been done for him. However, the best definition of customizing is "making the thing the way

Government surplus stores are a good place to shop for customizing material. Here a breathing oxygen container, with regulator valve, holds compressed air on this custom job and operates an air cylinder to open and close the hood and trunk at the press of a button. The air tank is refilled at a service station.

you want it." So if you don't feel like blindly following someone's lead, strike out for yourself.

Model Kits Are a Big Help

But if you do, avoid bankruptcy and continual rework by shaking down your ideas before you start. There is a model kit for just about every car made, even back to the Model T. Use clay, paper, balsa wood, and wax to work out your ideas on the model. Paint and repaint with different combinations. Change and alter so that your radical views can be inspected in three-dimensional form. Something that looks good from a front view may look like a nightmare from the side.

Don't dismiss the idea of working with models as "kid's stuff." In the end, a shakedown of ideas by working on models may separate the men from the boys when the custom coupes charge down the concrete.

11

DRAG AND STOCK

Hot rodding cuts across a wide field, but in the minds of the general public it is always tied in with drag racing. Dragging —acceleration tests—has been associated with our sport from the beginning. It started with street dashes that aroused such public ire, and then moved on to the famous dry-lake meets.

Today drag racing is still very much a part of hot rodding, but unfortunately it has moved away from the teen-agers who started it into hands of businessmen. Drag racing is not only a business, but a big business. It is no longer a participant's sport, but has become a spectator sport. More than eleven million paying customers bought tickets to see drag racing last year.

Drag Racing and Fuel

Big-time drag racing has been taken over by the fuel dragsters. It may seem that all cars burn fuel. That's true if you define fuel according to Webster. According to hot rodders, it is not gasoline but a nitromethane and methanol combination of exotic mixture.

The racers themselves have been modified until they no longer resemble an automobile. The driver sits out in a compartment moved so far to the rear that it looks like he's being left behind. The chassis, striving for the lightest weight possible, is nothing but rails. Naturally the setup is called a rail dragster. The backseat-driver position supposedly was invented by famed racing driver Mickey Thompson to put as much weight on the rear wheels as possible which improved traction.

Hot rod mechanics are tuning their engines right up to the moment of the race.

In this slingshot dragster the driver sits "out back" to increase traction by putting his weight over the rear wheels. Such vehicles are built specially for drag racing and can be used for nothing else. They represent the very top performance in the sport.

Combined with blowers, the nitro-combination fuels outperform any gas buggy. Once the National Hot Rod Association tried to ban them entirely, but fuel fans just turned to the American Hot Rod Association and Independent strips. NHRA gave in and fuel returned at the organization's 1963 Nationals. Speeds moved up and passed the 200-mph mark. Elapsed times began to split between eight and seven seconds. Then in 1966 John Mulligan was the first to break the seven-seconds barrier. He posted a 6.95 seconds e.t. at 221.12 mph. Drag racing was the world's fastest ground sport.

Such speeds brought increased accidents. Safety rules were tightened. The United Drag Racers Association decided that drag racers should pass an FAA pilot's physical examination. This, I suppose, was a belated acknowledgment that drag racing had become the next thing to flying.

Classes in Drag Racing

This kind of activity runs into money. The best brakes can't stop cars at this speed. Taking a tip from the drag chutes used on modern jet fighters, dragsters put parachutes on the rear of their slingshots to slow them down to the point where brakes could take over. They turned to magnesium for bodies. Mills were ginned up until they turned out 1,500 horsepower. Pistons, rings, rod, valves, cams, cranks, rings, and cylinder heads were all specially built for racing. Now we are talking about financial outlays from $10,000 to $15,000 to participate in a sport that began with $25-to-$50 Model A's. This cost not only eliminates teen-agers who started the sport, it also eliminates everybody else who does not have financial backing. The Top Fuel Eliminator class in hot-rod dragging is strictly professional today.

Those who don't have a minimum of $10,000 to gamble on hitting in the Top Fuel Eliminator grouping can join the semi-pros in the Junior Fuel Eliminator class. Here you can buy your way in with something like equipment running around $4,000.

Junior Fuel Eliminators are smaller-scale fuelers, lighter and unblown.

Gasoline, of course, is still around and the gas classes are

A Cougar takes off with spinning wheels for a trial run on the Orange County Drag Strip. The twin 'chutes on the back help this dragster stop at the end of the quarter mile run.

divided into quite a number of divisions. You'll find such things as Stock Class, Modified Production, Factory Experimental, Modified Sports, Altered Coupes, Competition, and so on. I never counted them myself, but somebody once said there are 27 separate classes you can enter in drag racing.

The Street Class Is Where You Start

Beginners should confine themselves to the street class. The best advice anyone can give you is to pick the division in your class where your limited means will not handicap you. I know one hopeful who consistently raced above his class. He never got anywhere. On the other hand, the smart ones start lower and work themselves up. A very interesting story of how a beginner can start with nothing much and use skill

Technical inspectors give each entering car a careful check to determine its class. After the inspection shows that no illegal equipment or modifications have been made, the car's class and entry number are painted on the glass. This "Swingin' Swinger" is powered by a 340-cube MoPar mill.

and guts to climb to the very top can be found in a book called *King of the Dragsters*, the life story of Don "Big Daddy" Garlits (Chilton Book Company, Philadelphia, 1967).

Garlits' story shows as nothing else can that if you have what it takes you can climb to the top. There is no better inspiration for a beginner in drag racing than to study Garlits' book.

The NHRA Street Section is divided into a number of divisions, but mainly this class is for cars that can be driven on the street. This rules out a lot of expensive racing goodies and gives the beginner a half-chance. Alterations are limited. Classes within divisions are determined by dividing a car's weight by total cubic-inch displacement.

There is not much point in discussing NHRA sanctioned drag-racing classes or rules. They are subject to change. For example, as this is written word comes that Wally Parks, NHRA president, has just announced major changes for 1970.

Professionals and Amateurs

According to Parks, racing competition will be divided in 1970 into a professional class and an amateur class. There will be no handicapping in the pro class, but the amateur group will all be handicap races.

Eliminator categories have been redesignated into two groups:

Group One—Top fuel, top gas, funny car and a newly formed pro stock car class.

Group Two—Competition, modified competition, super-stock and stock eliminator. The street class has been merged with the modified.

If there are no clubs around you that are affiliated with NHRA, you can get a copy of the latest rules and classes from the association's headquarters. Write them at 3418 West First Street, Los Angeles, California, **90004**. The price is about a dollar for the 1970 edition.

One thing to note is that the classes listed may not all be run in your locality. As a general rule, affairs that beginners can get in on are more frequent in the East than in the West. Geographical divisions are more important than one would think. In the West drag racing is king. In the Southeast there is more emphasis on stock-car racing.

Stock-Car Racing Is Different

It is hard to compare drag racing with stock-car racing. From a spectator point of view, stock-car racing provides more thrills. Here one sees a mass of cars fighting against each other. In drag racing you see two cars competing against each other and the clock.

By its very nature stock-car racing is more dangerous than drag racing, but not as much as the uninitiated may think. Occasionally one reads of spectacular pileups. Even then, injuries are surprisingly low. In one race the driver plowed into a guardrail. Metal crumpled like wadded paper. It seemed the driver didn't have a chance, yet he walked away without a scratch.

Followers of stock-car racing will tell you truthfully that you are safer on the race track than on the average freeway. This doesn't sound reasonable, but here is the way one driver put it:

"On the track you are driving with pros. You know what to do when squeezed into a corner and things get hairy. The other driver knows also. When you see trouble building up, you can predict what the other car will do. On the freeway there is nobody's crystal ball that can give an idea of what some of those mad clowns will do in a pinch."

There is a lot of truth in this. However, I think the extraordinary safety record of stock-car racing is due as much as anything to the National Association for Stock Car Auto Racing (NASCAR), the world's largest sanctioning body for stock-car races. The association's seemingly endless list of "don'ts" have gone a long way toward keeping racers alive and the sport healthy while still maintaining its exciting flavor.

As stock-car racing started out, there was no national body to enforce rules. Somebody with access to open land would lay himself out a dirt track, or promoters would make a deal with local fairs. Drivers entered whatever they wished. Safety was up to them.

Then after World War II racing resumed with a bang. Hot rodding became big business. More powerful cars rolled off the assembly lines in Detroit, and skilled owners made them even more powerful. Stock-car racing was viewed by the public in general as only slightly more respectable than drag racing. At this point, just as NRHA started bringing order out of the drag-race chaos, NASCAR was formed to direct the sport.

This was in 1948. In the past twenty-two years NASCAR has grown from an initial membership of less than 900 to something like 15,000. NASCAR sanctioned races number more than 2,000 with prize money exceeding $4,000,000.

Spectators total somewhere around 14,000,000. This tops drag racing attendance by a healthy three million.

In the Big Time

Officials now claim that automobile racing is the nation's number two sport, outdrawing football, baseball, and everything except horseracing. This, of course, includes all types of automobile racing from rolling over the bricks at Indianapolis to dragging at a local strip.

From the standpoint of the beginner, NASCAR Nationals are something to read about and see. They are strictly big-time racing today. These races draw the finest drivers and the best cars that money and ingenuity can produce. Few drivers themselves can afford the kind of car it takes to drive to the winner's circle in the Nationals.

Just shelling out ten thousand dollars and up for a car is only the beginning. There's the matter of a pit crew. All the winning of a race is not done by the man behind the wheel by any means. The real winner is a *combination* of driver, car, and pit crew.

Maintenance costs are terrific. These top cars are completely rebuilt after each race. The owner can spend more for tires in a single year than the street jockey spends on his entire heap.

Add to this the costs of following the NASCAR circuit around the country. If you go into this kind of racing seriously, it is a full-time job. You can't pump gas in a filling station all week and drive the Nationals on Sunday.

The circuit riders always hope to bring home enough "gold" to keep gas in the car and the wolf from the door. However, take a look at the winners' list. Nobody comes in first, or even second or third, all the time. A tire goes. A rod blows. You get caught in a pinch and have to take the escape road. Instead of getting gold you come home in the cold.

Getting a Sponsor

The way to get by is to have a sponsor. You'll never pick up a top industrial sponsor until you're a champion or near to it. The big automobile companies are after winners for their advertising value. It does not help the sale of cars to come in with the also-rans.

A lot of car owners can't drive their own vehicles. This is either because they lack what it takes or have reached the age where slow reflexes pull down their efficiency. They need drivers. However, if you drive somebody else's car, 60 percent of the winnings go his way.

It was Dave Pearson, 1966 NASCAR Grand National champ, who racked up $59,600 in winnings that year. His take of the gold was only $23,940. However, testimonials and endorsements and such sidelines gave him considerably more. Even so, this is not a large return for a year's grind.

An owner's cut seems large, but it really isn't. He foots the bill not only for the car but for the crew and its expenses as well. His chances of making a wad are about as good as if he had thrown the money on the tables at Las Vegas. Some hit it big. Most get only the fun of playing for their money.

Money, of course, isn't everything. Judging by the number who end the year with less than they started, it may not be anything. What does draw them is the spirit of competition, the love of big revving motors, and hope.

Why Enter Stock-Car Racing?

So, if you can't break in as a beginner and can't afford it even if you could be admitted to the charmed circle, why are we talking about stock-car racing in a book for beginners?

We are talking about it simply because if you want badly enough to hit the big time, you can—eventually. NASCAR knows very well that every driver on its circuit started out as a car-loving kid who grew into hot-rodding teen-ager and then into a potential NASCAR champion. As racing grows, so must the number of contestants. There has to be a training ground—a practical school where drivers can get experience and work their way up to the big time.

So there are classes to give everybody a chance. The Grand National is the top. Next in line is the Modified Circuit, which is split into two divisions. At the present time this is for 1935-64 and for 1956-to-1964 models. The latter is known as the Late Model Modified Division.

Next in line of prestige is NASCAR's Sportsman Division, where drivers with their eyes on the top goal can get experience and training. Here we see cars in the $4,000 class, which is still too much for an unsponsored beginner.

This division is also split into two classes. Like the Modified circuit it has a regular Sportsman class and a Late Model division. Cars are smaller in these classes than in the top divisions.

Hobby Division

Now we come to where the beginner gets into the act. This is NASCAR's Hobby Division. Here amateurs compete against amateurs. The pros from the other divisions are barred. Like the professional divisions, the Hobby Division is split into classes. They are:

Hobby Class
- Limited to American-made cars from 1936 through 1959.
- Engine displacement cannot exceed 318 cubes, and overbore must not be over .060 inch.
- Overhead valve engines limited to one carburetor. Flatheads may use two.
- Cam grind is optional.
- Quick-change rear ends, supercharging, fuel injection, and special intake manifolds are illegal.
- Stock transmissions only.
- Reinforced suspension required.
- Wheels may be interchanged, but must be passenger type.

Late-Model Hobby Class
- For passenger cars from 1955 through 1959. American-built only.
- Engine displacement vary with types. As examples, 1955-through-1957 Fords are limited to 312 cubes; '58 and '59 Fords can go up to 352; Mercury, same; Chevrolets, '55–'57, 283, '58–'59, 348, etc.
- Carburetion—limited to one four-barrel carb.

- Stock only for heads, valves, and intake manifolds.
- Along with the decals and fancy paint, you have to find room on the hood for the word HOBBY in letters a foot high.

Cadet Class
- Limited to 1953 through 1959 hardtops of American manufacture.
- Stock engine for the make and model raced.
- Carburetion: Four-barrel permitted.
- Any camshaft except a roller tappet.
- Locked rear ends are okay, and you have your choice of gear ratios.
- Four-speed manual transmissions are out, but any other stock transmission may be used.
- It is also legal to move the three-speed manual shift from the steering column to the floor.

These restrictions were in force when this was written, but as with all rules, somebody can change them tomorrow. Then you can add on some tough safety regulations besides. NASCAR wants to bring its drivers back alive.

Other Restrictions

You must have two seat belts, and shoulder harness is mandatory. The seat belts must be of the quick-release type and be at least three inches wide.

Roll bars are required and must be at least 1¾ inch outside diameter and welded. If the seat is adjustable, it must be bolted down so it will not move in an accident. Padding of the door on the driver's side is another requirement, as is padding of the steering post.

Lights, front and back, must be removed and the holes covered with metal. A tire-inspection hole can be cut in the floor, but otherwise the floor and firewall must remain untouched. You are also required to have positive fasteners on the hood and trunk lids to insure that they will not fly up at the wrong time.

NASCAR inspectors don't overlook anything. They demand a strap under the drive shaft. Then if the U-joint breaks, there is no possibility of the shaft digging into the track and flipping you in front of the other cars. Likewise, a scattershield is mandatory for the clutch and flywheel. They want it to be ⅜-inch steel.

Fuel cells are mandatory instead of gas tanks, and there must be a firewall between them and the drivers. And every car must have a fire extinguisher in the cockpit.

NASCAR was born in the Southeast coast states and is still strongest there. The Pacific Coast Division was not organized until 1954. Although sixteen years old, it has never been the dominating factor on the West Coast that it has been on the East. Up to the time this was written, the Pacific Coast Division does not sponsor Hobby Class Races. However, the Riverside International Raceway has amateur driver courses in the basic techniques of race driving.

Hobby Class races run from 20 to 30 laps over regular NASCAR tracks. This puts the drivers through a fast 10 to 25 miles. On runs like this a trained pit crew is not as essential as it is on the big 500-milers. Cars on the circuit cost as little as $150, but they have been plenty good enough to boost their drivers into the Sportsman Class.

Moving Up in Stock-Car Racing

Driving in stock-car races is a different job from handling a drag racer. Also, driving oval tracks differs from road racing. Dirt tracks call for different driving techniques than on asphalt. All this has to be learned on the tracks themselves. Reading, talking with pros, and watching races as well as working in the pits teach a lot. But there is no substitute for grinding around the track.

As experience grows, the beginner moves up from the Hobby Class into the Sportsman Divisions. He's in bigger time now. He's still running on the ½- to ⅝-mile tracks that he began on, but the events have moved up to 40 to 50 laps. Occasionally a special will run as much as 100 miles. Minimum prizes for first jump from $100 to $350 and up to as much as $1,000. A driver who can win consistently will be able to follow the circuit—something the hobby driver cannot afford.

Better machines, of course, are essential in the Sportsman Division. Where the Hobby Class may average $500 per car, in the Sportsman Division we start talking in the $3,000-plus range. For the beginner this sounds like a fantastic sum, but serious drivers may grind through five races a week. The shorter races do not take the toll on his machine that the Grand Nationals do.

From the Sportsman Division the next lap for the ambitious driver is the Modifieds. This comes closer to true hot rodding than anything else on the NASCAR circuits. On the Grand National run you can't get anywhere unless you have a rich backer and an automotive engineer in your pit crew. The Sportman and Hobby divisions are narrowly limited in what you can do to your mill. In the Modified—but not the Late Model Modified—there is much more freedom in putting your own wild ideas into your mill.

Greater Freedom of Choice

There is no weight-to-displacement requirement on Southern tracks, and Northern ones ask only for a minimum weight of 2,400 pounds. You can bore, stroke, or mill to your heart's content. Nobody cares what kind of engine you put in which kind of body. You can use carbs or fuel injection. You can shift the engine if you think that helps your weight distribution. Special cylinder heads, wild cams, pet manifolds, and your favorite pistons are also allowed.

You can also indulge your fancy about the ignition. However, they do insist on a starter. No pushing. You got to get to the line under your own power.

No kiddie-kars allowed. Modifieds must have started life with at least a 109-inch wheelbase, and no fair ripping off the fenders. As a concession to those who must drive every race to make ends meet, you are permitted to drive the next two events after you knock off a fender. After that it is back to the body shop or so long, Joe.

As with the other classes, safety regs are strict. A NASCAR inspector is right there to see for himself before you get on the track.

12
SUMMING IT UP

How does a beginner begin?

There are many ways. Some get a car, a book, some tools and start. Others, fortunate enough to find hot-rod clubs in their neighborhood, have sympathetic companions to help them get started. If there isn't a club, how about starting one? It is a rare young man who isn't interested in car, and it is not hard to get a club started.

An advantage of a club is that members can pool their slender budgets to build a better competition car than any of them could do alone. If you're good enough, who knows —the winnings may be enough to raise you up to a hotter class.

A really excellent place to start is in a high school automobile repair shop. Here the entire class can contribute toward a rod. Students of Western High School in Buena Park, California, recently exhibited at a Los Angeles Custom Car Show their beautiful 283 Chevy which they built in class and intend to race in the AA/fuel class in 1970.

Still another way to get started is to volunteer for pit work with established racers. The really big timers have professional crews, but a lot of semi-pros depend upon their friends to help them out. These, because of the necessity of making a living, aren't always around for every race. Maybe you could fit in as a spare in the beginning.

Actually building your own car is but the beginning. If you really love cars—and you must to devote the money and time that hot rodding demands—hot rodding may be the turnpike that leads you to a life profession. Youthful hot rodders

High school students gather around this station wagon, powered with a 409-cubic-inch engine, which their class has entered in the Ford Scholarship Race at the Orange County International Raceway in California. This Ford Motor Company event brought entries from 38 high schools in the county, attesting to the acceptance of modern drag racing by school officials.

have climbed to Indianapolis driving. Mickey Thompson, the speed king, was a hot rodder. Others, like Isky Iskanderian, Wally Moon, and Stu Hilborn turned to manufacturing speed equipment. Others became mechanics, owners of garages, high-performance experts for automobile dealers, race-track owners and promoters, free-lance writers, editors and publishers of car and rod magazines, and even presidents of hot-rod associations. Others operate specialized machine shops, run speed-equipment stores, and teach in automobile trade schools.

Become a Good Mechanic First

One thing is certain: if you are serious about hot rodding and a future in any phase of automobile work, you can't learn too much. The old days are gone when all a mechanic

Summing It Up   163

had to learn was the difference between a wrench and a pair of pliers. For a long-time automobile mechanics have been degenerating into parts-changers. There is today, garage owners tell me, an actual drought of good mechanics.

Being a good mechanic means more than just knowing what part to replace and how to tune up a car. You should know enough about it to design one of your own. This means knowing not only the practical nut-and-bolting, but also the theory behind it. In big-time racing and rodding it is surprising how many drivers and owners are college-trained. Knowing the physics and the chemistry behind an action can often mean the difference between adding and subtracting enough from a stock model to make it a winner.

Plymouth Trouble Shooting Contest

One of the best deals for a young man anxious to get ahead in his education is the Plymouth Trouble Shooting Contest. These contests are held every year in the spring.

This 283-cubic-inch Chevvy is the project of a high school class. It was built to compete in NHRA drag races. It is a beautiful job that shows what can be done through working together.

Contestants come from 2,000 high schools and junior colleges across the nation. Regional contests narrow down the candidates to 206 who comprise 103 two-man teams. For the last two years the National Finals were held at the Motor Speedway in Indianapolis. There is a LeMans type start. The 103 cars are parked on each side of the strip. The entrant teams line up. The announcer calls, "Gentlemen, start your engines!" as they do at the famous French track. Then he adds something never heard at LeMans: "*If* you can!"

The teams rush to their assigned cars. Each has six malfunctions and the troubles are all the same for each car. First to correct the malfunctions and get their car started are the winners. In addition to scholarships, the top five teams win complete Plymouth engines for their school automobile repair classes, and every competing team is given a complete set of tools for their school. Total prizes run $125,000. According to Plymouth, over 15,000 participants have gone on to become professional mechanics since the contest began in 1949.

If you are interested in a career in the automobile profession, hot rodding is a good way to start, but if you are only seeking fun, that's okay too. There is a thrill, a challenge, and a satisfaction that is hard to beat.

Good luck!

CAR CHATTER

Any activity gradually picks up a language of its own, and hot rodding is no exception. A host of new words have been introduced by drivers and mechanics. While common enough to the initiate, they are often bewildering to a beginner. Here are some of the more common.

Altered—A competition class which permits extensive modification but which requires an automobile body. No rails allowed.

Bent eight—a V-8 automobile engine.

Blower—supercharger. A **blown** engine is one equipped with a supercharger.

Bobbed—A vehicle body that has been shortened in customizing.

Bore—The diameter of the engine cylinder.

Bored—A mill that has had its cylinders enlarged (overbored) to give greater displacement. Displacement is the total volume. Boring permits more fuel mixture to be packed into the cylinders, increases compression, and adds to the power.

Bottom dead center—The lowest point a piston can move in a cylinder on the down stroke.

Boss—Tops; the best.

Cam—a camshaft.

Camshaft—A shaft drawing its motive power from the crankshaft, which has lobes that operate valve lifters which open and close an engine's intake and exhaust valves.

A **hot cam** is one specially ground to open and close the valves faster and keep them open longer.

Carb(s)—The carburetor. Also known as a **jug** or **pot**.

Channeled—Cutting the body to lower the overall height of a car. Once very popular. Today's low-silhouette cars do not need it.

Chopped—Cutting down the body top for a rakish appearance. Also going the way of channeling.

Christmas tree—The pole lights used to start drag races.

Chrondeks—Timing system used for drag racing.

Cubes—The cubic inches of cylinder displacement in a car engine. Determined from measurements from bottom dead center with cubes from all cylinders added together. When a company or rodder speaks of a 283 engine, he means one with 283 cubic inches of displacement—that is, 283 cubes.

Customize—To restyle a car in a distinctive manner.

Deuce—The 1932 Model A Ford—of fond hot-rodding memory.

Drag—An acceleration contest between two cars run over a quarter-mile track; 1,320 feet long.

Dragster—A specially designed drag-racing car.

e.t.—Elapsed time which is the time it takes for a drag racer to make the quarter-mile run. Electronic timers, graduated in milliseconds, start when the car leaves the starting line and cut off when it crosses the finish line at the end of the 1,320-foot strip. Elapsed timers do not clock the speed. Speed clocks check a 132-foot trap in the middle of the course.

Elapsed time—See above.

Exotic fuels—All racing fuels except gasoline; i.e., alcohol, nitromethane, etc.

Forked-eight—A V-8.

Fuel—High-performance mixtures with nitro base; fuels other than gasoline; exotic fuels.

Fueler (also *fuelie*)—Car that runs on exotic fuels.

Full bore—Wide open.

Funny car—Competition vehicles with altered wheelbase. Chrysler started "funny cars" in 1965 when it moved front wheels forward ten inches and the rear wheels forward 15 inches. This shifted weight to the rear end. The name "funny car" was pinned on them because the greater overhang in the rear looked odd. The name stuck. NHRA ruled them illegal, but as in the fuel ban, had to backtrack when funny cars caught on at non-NHRA tracks.

Goodies—Available additions to automobiles.

Hemi—Hemispherical, said of half-spherical combustion chambers. This shape permits use of larger valves. The Chrysler Firepower introduced in 1951 had a hemi-head engine. It created a sensation in hot-rodding circles.

Headers—The free-flowing first section of the exhaust.

Jug—Carburetor.

Mill (n.)—Engine.

Mill (v.)—To grind down a cylinder head along its mating surface in order to reduce the area of the combustion chamber and thus increase compression.

MoPar—Chrysler parts or products.

NASCAR—National Association for Stock Car Auto Racing—stock-car race-sanctioning body.

NHRA—National Hot Rod Association, sanctioning body for drag racing.

OHC—Overhead cams.

OHV—Overhead valves.

Pot—Another name for carburetor.

Rail—A dragster usually, although dune buggies often have rail bodies.

Rake—When one end of the car is lower than the other.

Relieved—When intake valve ports are cleared of metal obstructions.

Roll bar—Bent metal bars or tubes over the driver's seat to protect him if the car rolls over. If they completely enclose the driver's compartment they are called a **roll cage.**

SAE—Society of Automobile Engineers—Sets technical standards, for example, SAE-20, a grade of motor oil.

Scattershield—Protective shielding about the clutch or flywheel.

Slicks—Drag-racing tires with soft rubber surfaces instead of tread; give maximum traction during hard acceleration.

Cheater slicks have a slight tread cut into the soft surface.

Stock—Stock car, company production model.

Street rod—Car reworked for higher performance in ordinary driving. Moderate hot rodding. May also qualify for moderate drag racing.

Stroke—Distance piston travels inside cylinder; also, reworking crankshaft to increase the stroke of an engine.

Stroker—Mill that has been stroked.

Swap—To change engines.

T-bone—Model T.

Top eliminator—Class winner in drag racing. Last entrant left after others have been eliminated.

Wedge head—Wedge-shaped combustion chamber.

Wheelstand—When front end lifts as car comes off starting line, due to rapid acceleration and weight shift to rear.

SOME BACKGROUND BONING

In books this short it just isn't possible to put down everything a beginner should know about internal combustion engines. For this reason it may be necessary for you to seek additional specialized knowledge. The best place to get it is from an experienced mechanic. When this isn't possible, then your school or public library is your best friend. To help you here, we'll list a few books that should prove most helpful.

For general knowledge about internal combustion engines the various motor manuals are invaluable. No one can know everything, and even the expert has to seek a little "book learnin'" occasionally. When they do, you'll often find them using these books:

GENERAL

    Audel's Automobile Guide. Theodore H. Audel Company.

    Audel's Foreign Auto Repair Manual. Theodore H. Audel Company.

    Auto Engine Tune Up. Theodore H. Audel Company.

    Automotive Mechanics Principles and Operation. J. J. McGuffin. The Macmillan Company.

    Motor's Auto Repair Manual, 1970. Motor Magazine. (covers only 1963 through 1970 models.)

Automotive Fundamentals. Frederick C. Nash. McGraw-Hill Book Company.

CARBURETION AND IGNITION
Automotive Fuel and Ignition Systems. Irving Frazee. American Technical Society.
Transistor Ignition Systems Handbook. Bruce Ward. The Bobbs-Merrill Company, Inc.

CUSTOMIZING
Car Customizing, edited by Henry G. Felsen. G. P. Putnam's Sons. (An excellent primer on car customizing for beginners. It contains articles by various specialists in the field.)
How to Build a Fiberglass Car. Floyd Clymer. Floyd Clymer Company.

The above books are all authoritative, written by experts and published by leading publishers. They were chosen not only for their expert treatment of their subjects, but also for their clarity. However, they do treat their subjects in a general manner and often the beginner will want specific information on a certain car.

Here the best recourse is the manufacturer's manual for that particular car. All internal combustion engines are basically alike, but exact details and tuneup procedures as well as methods of dismantling and reassembly will vary widely from model to model. The shop manuals explain these changes. In addition to shop manuals there are books published on specific models of the more popular cars. Such books are available on Chevrolets, Fords, Plymouths, Dodges, Volkswagens, and some models of foreign cars.

To get such books, first try the local library. Most libraries are affiliated with an interlibrary loan system. When they do not have a book, they can borrow it for you from other libraries in the state.

Even more important than books for keeping up-to-the-minute on new developments is reading magazines. For the hot rodder two of the best are *Hot Rod* magazine and *Popu-*

lar Hot Rodding. They are both available at all large newsstands.

In addition *Hot Rod* magazine also publishes a line of extremely valuable "one-shot" magazine-type books featuring various hot rod specialties. One published last year on automobile chassis is splendidly complete. The books listed above treat the subject of automobile repair in general. They are essential to understanding your engine and provide the foundation for hopping up your engines. They are not hot-rod manuals in themselves. The magazines and specialized soft-cover books deal directly with hot-rod problems and solutions.

Index

Index

A

Acceleration tests, 148
A-frame, 110
Altered class, 165
Altered Coupes Class, 151
American Hot Rod Association, 10, 150
Archimedes, 31
Arcing, 24
Atlantic Boulevard (Los Angeles), 8
Audel's Automobile Tune-Up, 54
Austin, 45
Automobile, invention of, 15-16
Automobile repair, 169-171
Automobile repair shops, 161
Auto Repair Manual, 59

B

Backfiring, 79
Battery, 22, 24, 54, 97-98, 111
Bent eight, 165; see also V-8 engine
Blower, 86-87, 150, 167; see also Supercharger
Blueprinting, 71-72
Bobbing, 165
Body-parts molding, 145-146
Body solder, 132
Body work, 134-136
Boring, 66-68, 73, 75, 76, 79, 86, 87-88, 91, 104, 160, 165
Bottom dead center (BDC), 17-18, 50, 165
Brake drum, 124-126
Brake fade, 124-125, 126
Brake friction heat, 124-127
Brakes, 38, 122-127; disc, 125-127; radiation of, 125; replacement of, 127
Brake shoe, 124
Brake size, 125
Bucket seats, 145
Buick, 51, 106
Bumping, 135-136
Bypasses, 97

C

Cadet Class, 158
Cadillac, 1, 109
California, hot rodding in, 8-10
Caliper disc brakes, 125-127; floating, 127
Cams, see Camshaft
Camshaft, 27, 75, 89, 90-95, 165-166; full-race, 93; grinding of, 91-94; removal of, 94; replacement of, 94; semi-race, 92; souping of, 19-20; stock, 91-92; types of, 92

175

Camshaft kits, 92, 94
Camshaft lobes, 94
Carb, see Carburetor
Carburetion, 79-85; increasing, 53, 92; multiple, 79-83, 93
Carburetor, 54, 71, 75, 79-85, 89, 112, 160, 167, 170; adjustment of, 83-84; cleaning of, 85-86; invention of, 16; remolding of, 83-84; souped up, 19
Carburetor jet, 77
Carstand, use of, 40
Carter AFB (aluminum four-barrel) carburetor, 83
Centrifugal weight action, 54
Chain hoist, 110, 112
Channeling, 129, 166
Chassis dynamometer, 84
Cheater slicks, 168
Chevrolet, Louis, 65
Chevrolet engine, Chevy II, 105; 283 OHV, 106; V-8, 58, 65
Chopping, 128-129, 132, 166
Christmas tree, 3-4, 166
Chrome, 132-133, 136, 145
Chrondeks, 166
Chrysler, "Firepower" engine, 1; hemi-head engine, 105; V-8 engine, 66; V-8 383 engine, 65
Citroen, 38
Clearances, 74
Clutch, 25, 38, 88, 112
Coil, 22-23, 24, 55, 90
Coil springs, 121
Collector pipes, 95-96
Combustion chamber, volume of, 64-66
Competition Class, 153
Compression, boring and, 62-69; gasoline and, 16-18, 78-79; increasing, 33, 50-51, 53, 61, 73; milling, 58; problems of increasing, 71; rough idling and, 38; spark plugs and, 98; supercharger and, 86; timing and, 28
Compression ratio, 44, 53, 88, 92; defined, 50; stroking and, 67-68
Compression stroke, 18
Compression test, 54-55
Compression tester, 56
Condensers, 23-24, 54
Contact points, 22-24, 102

Corum brothers, 9
Corvette, 142
Costs, 60-61
Cotton, as fiber glass reinforcement, 142
Crankpins, 25-26, 69
Crankshaft, 25-26, 67-69, 88, 90, 113, 168
Crankshaft journals, 61
Crankshaft pulley, 29
Cubes, defined, 50, 166
Curing, of fiber glass, 142
Customizing, 53, 60, 128-137, 166, 170
Cut-in speed, 91
Cycle of operation, 14; souping up of, 19-20
Cylinder displacement, 64-66
Cylinder holes, enlargement of, 62-67
Cylinders, 18-19, 53

D

Dashboard, 145
Dents, hammering out of, 134-136
Deuce, 166
Diagnostic oscilloscope, 55
Diagonal cutters, 45
Differential, 113, 115-116; locking, 116
Disc brakes, 125-127
Disc rotor warping, 127
Displacement, 50-51; boring and, 62; determination of, 64-66; stroking and, 67-68
Distributor, 22-24, 27-28, 54, 98-99, 102
Distributor cap, 99
Drag racing, 3-4, 148-155, 166, 168; amateur, 153; classes of, 150-151; National Hot Rod Association and, 10; professional, 150-151, 153; safety of, 155; as spectator sport, 148
Dragster, 166
Drag strip, 2-3, 84-85
Drive shaft, 112-114, 115, 158-159; shortening of, 113-114
Drive shaft vibration, 114
Dual-exhaust systems, 96, 97
Duryea, Charles, 15, 16

Index ○ 177

Duryea, Frank, 15, 16
Dynamometer, horsepower measurement with, 49

E

Elapsed time, 166
Electrodes, 22-23, 24, 99, 100-101
Engine, 3, 167, 168; balancing of, 88-89; blown, 165; blueprinting of, 71-72; compression, 16-18; drag racing, 150; flat-head, 55; four-stroke, 15, 16-18, 54; in-line, 19, 26; internal combustion, 16, 169-171; invention of, 15-16; measurement of, 107-108; mechanics of, 14; milling of, 56-58; removal of, 110-113; types of, 18-19; V-8, 55; V-type, 19; *see also* Supercharger
Engine analyzer, 55
Engine block, cracked, 37; inspection of, 74
Engine breathing, 87
Engine conversion cuts, 105
Engine head warp, 73-74
Engine noises, 37-38, 53
Engine swap, 68, 104-118, 168
Engine tune-up, 54-56, 101
Epoxy plastics, 134
Exhaust stroke, 18
Exhaust system, 37, 95-96, 109; reworking of, 53
Exotic fuels, 166

F

Factory Experimental Class, 151
Fade, 124-125, 126
Fan, 94
Fan pulley, 94
Federal Aviation Authority (FAA), 150
Feeler gauge set, 45
Fenders, 145, 160
Fiber glass bodies, 140-145
Fire extinguisher, 159
Firing order, 26-28
Flatheads, 3
Flywheel, timing marks on, 29

Ford, Henry, 1, 47, 51, 65, 140-142
Ford, early models, 56; Model A, 106, 130, 150; Model T, 1, 31, 47, 95; 302 V-8 engine, 64-65; V-8 engine, 65; V-8 OHV engine, 106; V-8 260 engine, 109
Forked eight, 166; *see also* V-8 engine
Four-bangers, 3
Friction heat, 124-125
Fuel, 75-79, 148-150, 166; in early automobiles, 15-16; hot, 76-77; nitro-combination, 148-150
Fuel cells, 159
Fuel dragsters, 148
Fueler, 166
Fuel-injection, 19, 86-87, 93, 160
Fuel Injection Engineering Co., 87
Fuel pump, 75
Fuel system, 75-79
"Funny" cars, 2, 153, 166-167

G

Gapping, 99-101
Garlits, Don "Big Daddy," 152
Gasket ring, 100
Gasoline, 76-79; antiknock rating of, 29; compression and, 16-18; high octane, 77-78; premium, 28; regular, 28; timing and, 28
Gasoline octane, 29
Gasoline vapor, 77-79
Glass fiber, *see* Fiber glass
Grand National stock car competition, 156, 160

H

Hacksaw, 45
Halibrand Engineering (Torrance, Calif.), 117
Hammer, bumping, 135
Hankins, Bob, 11
Headers, 96, 97
Head warp, 72-73
Hemi-head engines, 3, 167
High school shop classes, 161-163
Hilborn, Stu, 162

Hilborn fuel injector systems, 87
Hobby Class, 157-160
Hobby Division, 157-158
Hood, 145
Hopping up, 12
Horsepower, 19-22; boring and, 65-66; brake, 47-49; compression ratio and, 53; defined, 47; gross, 49; increasing, 47-50; net, 49; supercharger and, 86-87; taxable, 47-48
Horsepower-to-weight ratio, 104-105
Hot rod, cost of, 60-61; defined, 1-2; purchase of, 32-40; street, 52; street/strip, 6; types of, 6-7; see also street rod
Hot Rod, 10, 170-171
Hot-rod clubs, 161
Hot rodding, defined, 1-2; history of, 8-11; how to begin, 7-8, 161-164; new public image of, 10; safety of, 8; as spectator sport, 5-6
Hydraulic brakes, 124

I

Ignition circuit, 102-103
Ignition swtich, 98
Ignition system, 22-29, 75, 97-103, 160, 170; improvement of, 53; transistorized, 102
Ignition system check, 98-99
Intake manifold, 71, 75, 76
Intake stroke, 16-17
Intake valves, 70
Interior finishing, 139-140
Iskanderian, Isky, 162

J

Jug, see Carburetor
Junior Fuel Eliminator Class, 150

K

Kiddie-kars, 160
King of the Dragsters, 152
Kingpin, 121
Knee action, 121

L

Late Model Hobby Class, 157-158
Late Model Modified Division, 157
Late Model Sportsman Division, 157
Leading, 135
Leaf springs, 121, 122
Lights, 158
Linkage, nonprogressive, 81; progressive, 80
Lowell, James Russell, 71
Lowering, 129, 132

M

Maintenance costs, 155
Mag (magnesium) wheels, 120, 145
Magnesium bodies, 150
Magneto, 98
Male-molded method, 144
Manifold, 96; multiple carburetion and, 80-83; porting or enlarging of, 19
Mechanics, 162-163
Mercury, 56
Metal shrinkage, 136
Methanol, 148
Methyl alcohol (methanol), 77
Milling, 20, 56-58, 63, 68, 75, 76, 79, 86, 88, 160
Mills, see Engine
Modified Circuit, 156-157
Modified competition, 153
Modified Production Class, 151
Modified Sports Class, 151
Modified Sportsman Division, 157
Moon, Wally, 162
Mufflers, 96-97
Mulligan, John, 150
Muroc, California, 8-9
Mustang, 51; 302 V-8 engine, 64-65

N

National Association for Stock Car Auto Racing (NASCAR), 8, 52, 72, 154-160, 167
National Hot Rod Association (NHRA), 5-6, 10-11, 34, 97, 114, 150, 152, 153, 154, 167

Index ○ 179

Net horsepower, 86
Nitrobenzene, 77
Nitroethene, 77
Nitro fuels, 76-77, 87, 148-150
Nitromethene, 77, 148
Nylon, as fiber glass reinforcement, 142

O

Oil bath filters, 86
Oil seal, 95
Oil-wetted filters, 85-86
Oldsmobile, 26
Otto, Nikolaus August, 15
Otto engine, 15-16
Overcompression, 64
Overdrive, 118

P

Paint, checked, 139
Painting, 136-139, 146-147; preparation for, 137-138
Paint remover, 139
Paper-filter air cleaner, 85-86
Parachutes, 151
Parks, Wally, 153
Parting agent, 144
Pascal, Blaise, 124
Pearson, Dave, 156
Pinion drive gear, 116
Piston damage, compression and, 53
Pistons, changing, 20-22; crankshaft and, 25-26; high compression, 63; stroking and, 69
Pit crew, 155, 159, 160
Pitting, 24
Pit work, 161
Pliers, 45
Plymouth GTX, 51
Plymouth Trouble Shooting Contest, 163-164
Pneumatic tires, 119
Points, 22-24, 54, 99
Polishing, 87-88, 93
Popular Hot Rodding, 170-171
Porsche, 143
Porting, 73, 87-88, 93, 104

Pot, see Carburetor
Power stroke, 18
Preignition, 53, 59, 77, 88
Primary winding, 23, 102-103
Propeller shaft, see Drive shaft
Pro stock car class, 153
Punch, 62
Pushrods, see Valve lifters

Q

Quad, 81
Quick-change rear end, 117-118

R

Racing recaps, 120
Racing tires, 120, 167-168
Radiator, 37, 94, 110
Rail, 167
Rail dragster, 148
Rake, 167
Rambler American engine, 49-50
Rear end, see Differential
Rear-end gears, 116
Rear-end overdrives, 118
Rear-end ratio, 116-117
Recapped tires, 120
Relieving, 73
Ring gear, 116
de Rochas, Alphonse Beau, 15, 16
Roll bar, 158, 167
Roll cage, 167
Rotor wobble, 127
Rubbing block, 23
Rust, 138

S

Safety, 8, 114, 158; in garage, 40-43
Safety loop, 114
Safety rules, 9-10, 150, 154
Safety Safaris, 10
Sanding, 138-139, 144-145
Scattershield, 159, 167
Screwdriver, use of, 43, 45
Seat belts, 158
Seat covers, 146

Secondary circuit, 23
Secondary windings, 97, 102–103
Secondary wiring, 24
Sepulveda Boulevard (Los Angeles), 8
Service manuals, 58–59, 170
Shock absorbers, 119; adjustable, 122
Shoulder harness, 158
Show-car customizing, 129–130
Slicks, 120, 167–168
Slingshot dragster, 149–150
Society of Automotive Engineers (SAE), 48, 167
Souping, 12
Southern California Timing Association (SCTA), 9–10
Spark, advanced, 28
Spark-plug gap, 99
Spark plugs, 22–29, 53, 54, 98–101; cold, 100; hot, 100; selection of, 100–101; wiring, 54, 99
Sponsors, 155–156
Sports cars, 38
Sportsman Class, 159–160
Sportsman Division, 157
Spray paint, 136–139
Springs, 119, 120–122
Starter, 98
Steering column shift, 140, 145
Stock-car padding, 158
Stock-car racing, 72, 153–160, 168; getting a sponsor, 155–156; maintenance costs, 155; respectability of, 134; safety of, 153–154, 158; safety rules for, 160; as a spectator sport, 153, 155; tracks, 159
Stock Class, 151
Stock Eliminator Class, 153
Street class, 151–152, 153
Street rod, 52, 60–61, 85, 94, 95, 129, 168
Stroke, 16, 168; compression, 18; exhaust, 18; intake, 16–17; power, 18
Stroking, 62, 66, 67–71, 73, 75–76, 79, 86, 87–88, 91, 104, 160, 168
Stroking kits, 69–70
Supercharger, 20, 86–87, 165
Super Stock Class, 153
Supertuning, 12
Suspension, 53, 119–129

Swapping, 131, 168
Swept volume, 56, 67–68

T

Tachometer, 145
Tappets, see Valve lifters
Thompson, Mickey, 148, 162
Timing, importance of, 24–28
Timing chain, 94, 95
Timing light, 54–55
Timing marks, 29
Tires, 119–120, 167–168; racing, 120; wide-tread, 145–146
Tire tread, 119–120
Tools, purchase of, 44–46; rental of, 46; use of, 40–46
Top dead center (TDC), 16–18, 25, 26, 29
Top eliminator, 168
Top Fuel Eliminator Class, 150, 153
Top Gas Class, 153
Torque, 62; rating, 62
Torque tube drive shaft, 113
Torsion bar, 122
Toxic vapors, 42
Traction, 119–120, 148, 167–168
Transistorized circuits, 102
Transmission conversions, 140
Transmission gears, 116–117
Tune-up, 54–56, 101; equipment for, 55–56

U

United Drag Racers Association, 150
Used car, purchase of, 32–40

V

Vacuum-advance, 28, 54, 99
Valve-lifters, 27, 90, 94, 99
Valves, 75; action, 27; balancing of, 88–89; clearance, 54; grinding of, 88; timing of, 94–95; tuliped, 64
Valve springs, 27
V-8 engine, 19, 26, 51, 55

Velocity stacks, 19
Venturi, 77, 85
Venturi, G. B., 77
Vibration dampener, timing marks on, 29
Volkswagen, 48, 128, 143
Voltage, 97-98, 102

W

Watt, James, 47
Wedge head, 168
Weight, horsepower and, 104-105

Welding, 134, 136
Wheel covers, 125
Wheels, 120
Wheelstand, 168
"Wonderful One-Horse Shay," 71
Work space, 40
World War II, effect on hot rodding, 9
Wrench, ignition, 45; spark plug, 45; torque, 45; use of, 40-43, 45

Z

Zoomies, 96

I. G. EDMONDS started tinkering with cars when he was ten years old, trying without notable success, he says, to make a 1923 Model T run. While this initial interest in cars never flagged, he never took an interest in racing and competition until 1953, when General LeMay opened March Air Force Base, near Riverside, California, for an annual sports car race on the air base ramps. Then in the Air Force, from which he retired as a Chief Master Sergeant after twenty-one years, Mr. Edmonds went to the races only because he was ordered to help. After that, he couldn't be kept away.

After serving combat tours in World War II and the Korean War, Mr. Edmonds spent three years on the news staff of *Pacific Stars and Stripes,* the military newspaper in Tokyo. In the service and out, he figures, he has written more words for newspapers on cars and racing than there are bricks at Indianapolis. Today he is with the public relations department of the Northrop Corporation, an aerospace company.

74 75 76 77 10 9 8 7 6 5 4 3 2 1